Renewal on the Run

# RENEWAL
## ON THE RUN

*Encouragement for wives who are partners in ministry*

# Jill Briscoe

### foreword by
### Stuart Briscoe

Harold Shaw Publishers
Wheaton, Illinois

Some material has been adapted from messages given by Jill Briscoe at leadership conferences. For information on the 3-cassette tape series "Principles, Pressures, & Priorities of a Christian Partnership," write to: Briscoe Ministries, Elmbrook Church, 777 South Barker Rd. Waukesha, Wisconsin, 53186.

ISBN 0-87788-719-5

Cover photo © 1992 by Robert McKendrick

---

Library of Congress Cataloging-in-Publication Data

Briscoe, Jill.
    Renewal on the run : encouragement for wives who are
partners in ministry / Jill Briscoe.
        p. cm.
    Includes bibliographical refereneces.
    ISBN 0-87788-719-5
    1. Clergymen's wives. 2. Women in church work.
I. Title.
BV4395.B757 1992
253' .2—dc20                                    92-7913
                                                CIP

---

99  98  97  96  95  94  93  92

10  9  8  7  6  5  4  3  2  1

*To all the ministry wives*
*who have left marks of challenge*
*and service on my life—*
*footprints of faith.*

*You may well recognize your advice to me in these pages. May our words together encourage other women in our unique setting to aim high—to go for the gold—for he whom we serve is worthy!*

*Jill Briscoe*

# Contents

# Foreword

A famous cartoon depicts two donkeys with their tails tied together. In the first frame they are facing opposite directions, each avidly viewing a pile of hay. The second frame shows them pulling furiously in opposite directions, making no progress and subjecting their tails to intolerable strain. In the third frame they have recognized the futility of their approach and are sitting down discussing the problem, and in the final frame, with smiles of donkey delight, they walk together first to one pile of hay and then the other!

At the risk of being misunderstood, dare I suggest that some ministry marriages are not unlike our donkeys? No, I'm not suggesting that your churches work you like donkeys and feed you hay or that when the knot was tied the tails were knotted too! What I mean is that it is not uncommon to find ministry marriages that are being subjected to severe pressure. Both parties have needs and desires, priorities and expectations, but unfortunately they are found in opposite directions.

The marital partners are both pulling hard, but neither is getting to his or her bale of hay. Neither is truly satisfied, fulfilled.

The problem is made worse because they don't take time to sit down, talk, and listen. Sometimes this is because of busyness. More often it is a matter of reluctance, maybe unwillingness on the part of one partner to confront an awkward issue. Or it could be caused by a sense of guilt that they are not meeting human expectations or measuring up to divine standards. So they continue to pull and pull, managing only to tighten the knot and stretch their tails.

This book is designed to help ministry couples sit down, identify for each other their differing bales of expectations, and devise ways of reaching them together. I know this is a necessary exercise because Jill and I have strong convictions, lots of drive, and definite ideas, and we've done our share of pulling in opposite directions. But once we were prepared to recognize this and get on track together we achieved much more. And we found for each other and in each other much more than hay. We found gold, silver, and precious stones. I hope you will, too.

# Introduction

GOD HAS PURPOSES CONCERNING US
WHICH HE HAS NOT YET UNFOLDED; THEREFORE,
EACH DAY GROWS SACRED IN WONDERING EXPECTATION.
—*PHILLIPS BROOKS*

We ought to begin with a basic question: why a book especially for wives who are partners in ministry? The answer: for all sorts of good reasons!

*First of all, wives of men in the ministry constitute a growing portion of our population today.* There are currently thousands of women in America alone who fit in this category. For easier reading, I'll call them "ministry wives" throughout the rest of this book. Many of these women are married to pastors; others labor with their husbands in youth or missionary work, or in programs for the homeless, the addicted, the neglected, and the poor.

Some of these wives are living out the vision they have shared with their husbands since the beginning of their lives together.

Others married men who were in "secular" work and changed midstream to the enriching, yet challenging work of a ministry. But, as one wife informed me, "Second career ministry has its problems! And I'm not doing too well with mine."

Some ministry wives are serving by choice.

Others are in shock. They say such things to me as, "Oh! I never expected this!"

> Ministry wives have specific needs that are rarely touched in other books for women.

All of them have needs that are particular to people who work in a ministry. For years, pastors and missionaries have had conferences designed for their specific needs. I think it's time their partners had the same practical encouragement and help.

*Secondly, ministry wives have specific needs that are rarely touched in other books for women.*

I have been a "ministry wife" for thirty-three years. And I have had the privilege of knowing hundreds of wives just like me. We have grown and groaned together! I am familiar with many of our trials and our rewards.

Not only that, but through international conferences, I have had the privilege of gleaning wisdom from women who have shared a kaleidoscope of ministry with their husbands in a myriad of different places. All put together, we've amassed quite a storehouse of information. And we think it's time to make it available from the bookstore shelf.

If you are a ministry wife, know that these pages were composed lovingly with your needs, questions, struggles, and triumphs in mind.

*Thirdly, a book like this is necessary for another very large group of people—the husbands of ministry wives!*

A fact revealed by a survey taken by the National Association of Evangelicals (N.A.E.) is that one of the main reasons clergy are leaving the ministry by the hundreds is the stress placed on the clergyman's wife.

If you have an unhappy pastor's wife, you have an unhappy pastor, and it's time that more people got around to realizing that. Sometimes denominations or ministry organizations send pastors and their wives to "pastor" conferences, at which the pastors all go to sessions together. But their wives? Their wives get sent to the zoo or to a shopping mall! Well, I love to shop (I'm not so keen on elephants), but I can do all that at home. What I really think we ministry wives are looking for when we come to these conferences is substantial help in addressing some of the demands of *our* particular vocation.

> These pages were composed lovingly with your needs in mind.

To be a pastor's wife is not the same as being a pastor; to be a youth leader's wife is not the same as being a youth leader (although some expect as much). And it's not merely the same as being a wife. Ministry wives have a whole set of responsibilities, expectations, and stresses attached to their role. And we don't learn how to deal with these issues by a form of osmosis, whereby we stick close to our husbands and hope that what they are being taught will somehow trickle into our gaps of knowledge. We need help pertaining to our unique opportunities and wisdom to know how to release the pressure.

By the time a couple leaves a ministry, there is often great damage done to that marriage and to those individuals. Thus, this has the potential of being a very "down" book, because we must face our stresses and our hurts, talk about them, try to deal with our anger, and do some grieving together.

But the title of this book is not "Why ministry wives would not be ministry wives if they could do it over again"! I want to tell you that you're not alone! And I don't just mean "misery loves company." In Jesus' power and grace I believe we are able to resolve these deep conflicts and find healing and help. I know this to be true not only from my own journey of faith and ministry but from the countless stories of other people in the same boat, all over the world.

You see, I do believe the ministry wife's role is a privilege—not a punishment. It is not a prison sentence. If I were not convinced of this, I would put away this project right now.

> The ministry wife's role is a privilege, not a punishment.

The person living in the parsonage may have problems—but they are the problems of the privileged and can by and large be answered. There *is* real joy in living out God's focus for our lives. We ministry wives are indeed special people! Let's discover that real joy—together.

# 1

# Just Because I'm Me

AM I PRISONER OF PEOPLE'S EXPECTATIONS
OR LIBERATED BY DIVINE PROMISES?
—*HENRI NOUWEN*

Although the role of women has changed tremendously over the centuries, one fact has never changed: Jesus treated women with ultimate respect and honor. In a day in which women were considered second-class citizens, he took the time to minister to them and meet their specific needs. He risked social ostracism by speaking with the Samaritan woman at the well; he healed the woman with the issue of blood. And, most of all, he allowed women to minister to him, instead of rejecting their services. Women were first at his birth, last at his cross, and first to run and tell of his resurrection. The Lord accepted Mary of Bethany's love and adoration as she emptied out her precious box of ointment over his feet. He also spoke up for her when even the disciples criticized her for her "wasteful" actions. We are told in Luke 8 that many prominent women traveled with him, ministering to his needs. Thus, Jesus ministered *to* women, *with* women, and benefited *from their ministry to him*.

The apostle Paul also shared his ministry with women and gave them lots to do. Without getting into hot areas of controversy concerning whether women should minister to men, we are quite safe in saying that the apostle Paul, at the very least, commended women to minister to women. That made a lot of sense in Paul's day and age, and it makes even more sense in ours.

> Jesus allowed women to minister to him.

Today, one of the heaviest arguments for why women should equip themselves to minister especially to women is the terrible breakdown of the family. One woman told me, "I have been terribly abused by a man and have come to ask your advice."

"Will you see one of our trained counselors?" I asked her.

"Do you have both men and women?" she countered.

"Yes," I replied.

"Then I'll see a woman," she said. "I've had it with men."

Understandably, she was not over-willing to counsel with someone of the opposite sex. She was, however, very open to listen to the encouragement of another woman. And this makes sense.

After all, who but a woman can feel the pain of a rape victim? And who but a mother can fully empathize with a young woman who is childless or has suffered a miscarriage or struggled with being shut up with small children all day long? Who but a woman can sympathize with the mercurial monthly emotions of PMS or the changes that come unbidden when we hit the age of fifty?

What a wide open door our very sex affords us. We can walk right into the hearts and lives of half the human race and present Christ, all because we are female—in fact, "Just because I'm me"! We should have no trouble being a channel of blessing wherever we live and work and play. But, as one ministry wife told me, "Before God's message can liberate other souls, the liberation must be real in me."

I find that women are creative, intelligent, innovative, sensitive, gifted, nurturing, resourceful, spiritual, capable, and very tough! God knows that's true because he made us. He intended that we should be all that we are and that all we know should be used to reach our world for him. But I believe that he particularly (though certainly not exclusively) intends for us to reach "our own."

At first I resented this very idea. When I first became a pastor's wife I shied away from the intimidating woman who invited me to be part of the "woman things" at church. To escape I chose to work with the teenage department—having gifts, love, and aptitude for this age group.

But my very position called for a certain amount of involvement in the small but good women's ministry in the fellowship. I began to see that being "the Pastor's wife" gave me an unprecedented chance to have impact and influence at the very heart of the church. There were—in my humble opinion— plenty of "down sides" to being in my position, but plenty of "up sides," too! Once I had told the Lord what he well knew already—that I didn't particularly enjoy being around women and that I didn't want to spend most of my time with that group—I was able to add that my heart was in his hands, and he had my full permission to change it. I left the situation there, but he didn't. He said, "Thank you, Jill," took my heart in his hands, warmed it with his own love for women, and led me into such an exciting adventure in women's ministry for the next twenty years that I'm still reeling!

> Women are creative, intelligent, innovative, sensitive, gifted, nurturing, resourceful, spiritual, capable, and very tough!

There is, indeed, a place for women in full-time or lay ministry, whether as single persons or in partnership with their spouses. Women were a palpable force throughout the text of the Bible, their decisions determining the destinies of nations, their willingness to serve God inspiring examples of humility and power (yes, these two qualities can go together!).

In their most excellent book, *Daughters of the Church: Women and Ministry from New Testament Times to the Present*, Ruth Tucker and Walter L. Liefield say in their introduction to the historical research, "We have found that women have been very active in a wide variety of ministries within the institutionalized church despite pronouncements and official decrees to the contrary." And "Women in evangelical churches have a long heritage of seeking (and sometimes obtaining) meaningful positions in the church for the purpose of serving God more effectively." I would also like to add that the ministry wife has a position already—simply because she is who she is! She is perhaps married to the youth director, and is already accorded for good or ill a position of privilege and a chance to make a difference for God and for his kingdom.

There *is* a place for you, ministry wife! There is a divine purpose underlying your day-to-day struggles and temptations. God has always had great plans for you.

*Why then,* some of you may ask, *am I so miserable? Why do I feel so purposeless and powerless and even "used"? Why will I do almost anything to find someone who* really *understands my needs?* Any ministry wife will feel that way at some point in her journey. I've heard much more desperate statements from women who looked the perfect outward example of efficiency and confidence.

> God has always had great plans for you.

Do you have any idea how many ministers or their wives are having extramarital affairs, even while being in positions of leadership? One current survey revealed that three percent of those surveyed were struggling in that area. A woman who was involved in an adulterous situation told me, "Sex is just a small part of the reason I'm having this affair." You will hear all sorts of reasons for unfaithfulness, but many of them, like that woman, can trace the problem back to basic loneliness and a lack of self-esteem, or the absence of a unifying theme to life with their spouses. The sense of "ministry" doesn't even rate in their thinking. Some very large needs are not being met. Too many women in ministry have never learned to live as if there really is a very special place for them, one ordained by God and treasured by him.

## "How Do I Know Where My Place Is?"

"That's all very well," you say, "That's not my problem. I want to know *where* my place is. Or *what* it is. Life gets more confusing by the minute. There are certainly enough people ready to tell me what I'm *supposed* to be doing, but I can't listen to all of them." Well, that's true. And certainly not all of them will be right. It's very possible that not a single one of them knows what's right for you. Your story is just that—yours. Your journey can be mapped out only by your own cooperation with the heavenly Father.

The place to start in knowing *your* place is in the Scriptures. By this, I don't mean that by reading a certain piece of holy writ you will know automatically whether or not to get some biblical training or which women's group (if any) to teach. I'm not talking about details yet. We need to get the general principles straight first. So let's see what the Bible has to say about the place of women— and therefore of ministry wives—in God's economy.

> There will always be people who want to tell you what your place is.

Psalm 139 tells us that God has searched and known us thoroughly. It says it's impossible to run away and hide from the Spirit of God (verses 7-12). It assures us God will be a light in our dark hours and a secure presence at all times (verses 10, 12). Verses 13-16 are wonderful words. Our loving Creator carefully crafted us according to the purpose for our existence. Even before we were born he was thinking about us and the days we have ahead. "*All* the days [not just some of them, and not just the good ones] ordained for me were written in your book before one of them came to be" (verse 16). The psalmist says these are wonderful thoughts. I would concur.

> We are handmade to be handmaidens for the Lord.

But Psalm 139 was not written for David alone. Nor was it written just for our husbands. It was written for all of us. We women are handmade to be handmaidens! He has ordained (set aside for himself) every twenty-four hours; how could our days ever be daily again? After reading this passage, I wrote in the margin of my Bible: *A clean page is turned in heaven every day—God has his pen in his hand; he's ready to write about me—how exciting!*

## "I Know What God Says, But He's Not the Only One Talking"

I can hear some of you saying, "My daily days don't seem ordained or special to me at all. It's all well and good to know where I stand in God's scheme of things theologically. But that doesn't solve my *practical*, day-to-day relationships and challenges. I live in a world of people and situations, and the enemy is always about, seeking to sabotage any good image of myself that I've acquired from God's truth." Well then, if that's the case, let's look at a few resources for the battle. In other words, where do we go for help?

### *A good self-image is nurtured by friendship.*
According to one fact-finding group, forty-four percent of pastors' wives have no trusted friend, and thirty percent have no person they could go to for support or any support group at all. But guess how many of those women asked for help when they really needed it? *One percent.* Only one percent

shouted, "Help!" even though they were hanging on by their fingernails. Why is this the case? There could be many reasons but maybe one of the chief ones is the shallow nature of the friendships that do exist for the ministry wife.

So many people in our churches are spiritually and emotionally starved. They drain us dry instead of charging us up. They have no real friendship to offer. And yet if there's anything a ministry wife needs, it's friendship. And I don't mean just the acquaintance who comes over for coffee or goes to the mall with you to peruse the sales. Meaningful friendships are part of God's design. Every person needs at least one close friend. This is especially vital in the ministry.

> Meaningful friendships are part of God's design.

For ministry wives, this can be tough. For instance, the wife of a minister is never viewed as being in the same category as "normal" people (a problem suffered also by her husband). Either people assume you are aloof, or they themselves act aloof. Not only that, but people in a congregation or some other ministry group feel very intimidated and vulnerable when they see weaknesses in their "leaders" and those leaders' spouses. They are a little afraid to know what's really going on in our lives, especially if it's ugly, or it hurts. Somehow they think we should be "above" problems.

For this reason, quite a few ministry wives have friends (if they have friends at all) outside their church or organization. Sometimes they are the wives of other men in ministry. Sometimes they are people with the same outside interests, such as literature, sports, or crafts. But, much of the time, the ministry wife, cloistered as she is in the unending cycle of activities and the demands of her family's needs, pursues no real friendships at all. She has been taught to expect that God will meet her every need.

Indeed, God does intend to meet all our needs. But he meets them through certain instruments, one of them being close and meaningful relationships.

I struggled with this in a youth mission situation because our leader's wife believed you shouldn't have close personal friendships on the "team." She felt, perhaps from experience, that it caused tensions and friction. Maybe since *she* didn't have a close personal friend, she thought that we wives didn't need one either. She was wonderfully able to live like that, but I wasn't. I tried very hard to be like her because I admired her and wanted to model after her. But I'm the sort of person who needs friends in order to operate at my best. As I looked at the Scriptures, I noticed that Jesus himself had friends: twelve good friends, three very good friends, and one best friend!

**Think about the circles of Jesus' friendships.** Jesus never apologized for his friendships, and that often got him into trouble, even among the twelve. He was always picking his three very good friends out of the crowd and not explaining why, and that inevitably caused envy and jealousy. Jesus modeled friendship because he chose to need it and knew that we all needed it, too. He knows that women especially need the friendship of other women.

> Jesus himself had friends.

So during that particular time in my life, I knew that I needed to get very practical about what I was learning about Jesus and his friendships. So I sat down at my kitchen table and drew three circles within each other: the outside circle for the twelve, the next one for the three, and the one in the center for his special friend. I prayed, asking the Lord which individuals, in my life, belonged in those circles. And then I drew another outer circle, beyond the twelve, this circle representing the seventy—Jesus' close aquaintances. Beyond that was the space representing the multitudes.

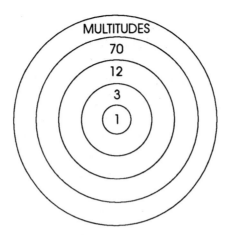

So what happened to me that day? As I wrote names in those circles I finally quit feeling guilty about having friends—about not spending as much time with my "seventy" as I spent with my "twelve" or as much time with the "twelve" as I did with the "three," and so on. As I was freed up to pursue friendships, many needs were met, and I was enabled to be a better (and less stressed) youthworker's wife.

**A close friend makes a big difference.** Why are friends so necessary? First of all, good friends know how to listen. They allow you to let off steam, to cry, to throw a temper tantrum. They help us to process our experiences, and to be truly honest. If the many unhappy ministry wives I've met could do one or two of those things on a regular basis, they would feel better immediately. I know I did!

At one point in our ministry when my husband had a period of heavy traveling, I found the friendship of one particular woman a lifesaver. Fortunately, I had been through the learning process I have just described and was able to be open to extending friendship to Angela. She was a true friend—leveling with me in love (and when you are leveled in love you are

> Good friends know how to listen.

never *leveled!*), "being there" in the tough and tender times in those early child-rearing days and, above all, making me laugh. The therapy of laughter, I discovered, happens easily between good friends, bringing release from tensions. She was also my sister, my partner in projects. Many times when we arrived home well past midnight exhausted yet happy after evangelistic efforts with youth, we drank a welcome cup of tea together. With Angela I found a friendship of equals that was quite a new experience for me.

| Good friends are accepting.

As I wrote in *Thank You for Being a Friend* (available from Briscoe Ministries), a book about my friendship with Angela and other women in my life: "As long as our friendship remained inclusive and not exclusive God enriched our lives and service immeasurably."

I found out that really good friends are accepting. Their world doesn't fall apart when your imperfections come glaring through. They don't have you on a pedestal to begin with, so when you fail or show weakness, their love and appreciation remain constant. Love isn't blind, I discovered. Only love sees.

Good friends tell you the truth about yourself. Most of the time they don't have to tell you the negative part of the truth; you are already overly familiar with your bad points.

No, a friend tells you repeatedly about your positives. She sees you through more merciful eyes than you see yourself.

| Good friends are cheer-leaders.

Did you know that many women in ministry are driven people—are high achievers? The personality profiles are often that of the type of person who is hard on herself, who is never satisfied. A good friend knows you well enough to tell you when it's time to "lighten up."

Friends are intent on encouraging, on being lifelong cheerleaders for each other.

A genuine friend can make quite a difference. So maybe it's time you prayed that God send you one. Maybe he already has, but you were just too self-involved to see it. That's easy to do. Perhaps there is a person right under your nose who would be amazingly good at reciprocating your love and support. We are so programmed to think that we must always be the givers, and others are to be the receivers. Take a fresh look at your present relationships and examine their potential.

> Take a fresh look at your present relationships and examine their potential.

You might not find a friend in your own church or team. That's not important. The important thing is to find a friend. Although the Lord sometimes brings each of us through periods of aloneness, even periods of friendlessness in order to teach us dependence on him, those states should only be temporary. We were meant to live in relationship to others.

### *A good self-image should be nurtured by your best friend—your mate.*

It should go without saying that your husband should become not only a good friend, but also a source of positive feedback for you, helping you to maintain a healthy image of yourself. But the sad truth is that many spouses are more detrimental to the self-image of their partners than they are helpful.

This is a large, complex area of relationships, and I won't attempt to address it fully here, but in more detail in Chapter 6. For now, we can remind ourselves of a couple of important principles.

**A husband saddled with the responsibility of being the sole source of his wife's ego will wither in a matter of weeks.** Wives can depend far too much on their husbands for their self-esteem, and that dependence generally has a boomerang effect. Spouses weren't designed to carry that kind of load alone. Therefore, it is imperative that women base their self-esteem on God and his Word and nurture it through other relationships besides the marital one—especially with other Christian women.

**A husband doesn't always know automatically what to do to bolster his wife's self-esteem.** Just as husbands and wives can't read one another's minds about other things, sometimes they haven't a clue as to what makes the other feel good about himself or herself. Maybe we need to be brave enough to tell each other what we need in this regard. Perhaps you need to say to your husband, "I need you to tell me I look nice!—especially when I'm pregnant!" for example. Sometimes spouses (this is especially true of newly marrieds) don't know enough of the other person's history to know what will hit a nerve. A lot of the hurts that occur within a marriage happen through ignorance. If you want your husband to join in this effort to help your self-image, he will need some specific information from you. You can't be afraid to reveal yourself to him. Nurturing each other's self-esteem happens by degrees; it will take time. But it can and will happen, if both of you put forth the effort. And that effort will reap benefits in many other areas of your marriage as well.

> It is imperative that women base their self-esteem on God and his Word.

I well remember feeling dreadfully inadequate in a group of what I used to call "ultra-suede ladies." (I couldn't afford to dress in such fashion.) Stuart always seemed to be relaxed in all the situations we found ourselves in, but not me. My mother had always told me, "The art of dressing well is to dress appropriately for the specific occasion." But that was the problem. As a "poor" ministry wife how could I dress appropriately, which—to my mind—meant like them? My self-image was all wrapped up in how I looked to others and not how I looked to Christ. As I relate in *Thank You for Being a Friend:*

"I found myself a guest in an incredible 'villa.' We were to change for dinner in a 'small' bedroom (about half the size of our entire house!). The other ladies were pouring themselves into their exclusive outfits and throwing around the casual remarks about Dior's latest show! It was my turn in the shower, and grateful for the respite, I spent so long in there my skin began to get quite waterlogged! Miserably reaching for the gorgeous bath towel and wondering momentarily if 'that' wouldn't look better than my dress, I tried tying it around myself 'sari' style. It was certainly cute and different, but I knew it wouldn't do and so reluctantly I had to emerge wrapped in the terrific terry cloth toga, with my little bit of starched cotton dress hanging limply from my hand. I was met by a fabulous-looking creature who remarked kindly, 'That looks like a pretty little creation, Jill.' She had focused the attention of the entire roomful of women onto my apparel. I didn't need to say it, but I did anyway. 'Sears,' I whispered, as if I'd just been caught shoplifting! *Why did I do that?* I asked myself furiously. *Why couldn't I just smile and say 'Thank you,' because it was a pretty dress and quite as lovely as all the rest, just not as expensive.* I knew in my heart, of course, that my reaction was a guilty confession to these women that because of the way I looked I felt totally out of place among them. At that moment it did not occur to me that when my Lord Jesus had stood in front of Pilate he wore his beautiful homespun garment instead of a Roman toga. How incongruous that would have been. His clothes hadn't stopped people from listening to him, that was for sure! How could it be that I still believed those ultra, ultra-suede ladies would only hear what I had to say if I dressed in ultra-suede? I don't know why I didn't reach back in my memories to our youth ministry years and remember I didn't dress in jacket and jeans to get the ear of the kids in the streets.

It was a little time later that God worked a miracle in my heart through his Word but mostly through Stuart's practical and humorous affirming help. It was after he had lovingly and teasingly made me feel like a million dollars that I was able to accept an invitation to Washington by the ultra-suede to talk to the ultra-suede! . . .

I was able to see that 'Just because I'm me' meant I was ideally matched for the occasion and opportunity—whatever I was wearing. This, of course, doesn't mean you dress like a dog, but you dress as suitably as you are able and get your mind off yourself and onto things that matter more. The bottom line was that God was able to assure me that I was ultra-suede in *his* eyes, and that settled it."

### A good self-image must be kept separate from particular issues.

One interesting thing I've learned by asking lots of questions is that pastors' wives in churches with memberships of under one hundred use words or phrases in their answers like *miserable, too much, want out, disappointed with myself, confused, depressed, down, my fault.* Pastors' wives in churches of over a hundred use words or phrases like *stretching, challenge, good, trying, want to do better, give me skills, give me practical help.* So I have come to the conclusion that the self-worth of the Christian leader and his wife is often wrapped up in what's happening in their work. "Numbers," for instance. "There must be something we should be doing to get more people to come," they say to each other. Sometimes a pastor's wife has confided to me despondently, "Maybe I'm the reason we're not growing."

> You are ultra-suede in God's eyes.

**There is a real tyranny in numbers—in counting heads.** Currently I serve a large church. But I have not always served in large churches or had great audiences. I am a native of England. Sometimes I would travel fifty to a hundred miles to speak to ten or twenty people in a church. I did that for years, so I know what it is to expend considerable energy to get somewhere and try not to count how many heads there are in front of me. It can be very discouraging.

> Try not to count heads.

As I've traveled the world and met ministry wives in every conceivable situation, I find that many of them are terrorized by numbers. How many people come to their women's group, for example. But the biggest help to me is that I have two daughters-in-law who are ministry wives. At the moment they are a huge source of joy, help, and inspiration. I am personally and prayerfully involved in watching and listening to my two girls who are probably very good representatives of the majority of ministry wives' situations. They are teaching me a lot, but they also struggle with the things I used to struggle with—numbers for instance.

When my eldest son, Dave, first told me he was taking a little church up in Menominee, on the upper peninsula of Michigan (a mile away from the North Pole, as far as I was concerned!), I said, "Menominee where, Dave?"

"It's a small town and at the moment somewhat economically depressed, Mom," he answered. "The shipyards are in trouble, and so many people seem to be moving out. It's also pretty rural outside the town itself."

That was four years ago. Over this period we would call him up and I'd say, "How's it going, Dave? How's the work progressing?"

And he would reply, "Well, Mom, on Sunday we had so many in church."

Then I would say, "Dave, I didn't ask how *many* you had in church. I asked, how's the *church* going?"

Numbers were something that as a young pastor he tended to take too much notice of. In Dave's mind, his worth and ability as a pastor seemed to be at stake, depending on how many turned up at church.

I remember my husband saying very wisely to him, "David, when you're thinking of church growth in an area like yours, to *maintain* is to grow." And that was a big help to David,

| Numbers never tell the whole story. | because that's where he was for a couple of years—at maintenance level. He learned not to let numbers affect him, and now God has graciously taken that congregation into a period of growth under his leadership. |

If you are in an area where jobs are being lost, and half the elderly people go to Florida for the winter, remember—"to maintain is to grow." Hang in there. "This, too, will pass!"

So, as a ministry wife, you must separate numbers from who you are and who your husband is. Numbers never tell the complete story, and sometimes the part of the story they do tell has nothing to do with the reason for your being there.

**The tyranny of prejudice and opinion.** I have often been asked how I feel about being referred to as "the pastor's wife." I don't mind at all myself, but this is a touchy issue for some women, and their objections are reasonable. After all, you don't generally introduce someone as the "garbage collector's wife" or as the "public accountant's wife"!

Although women in general have risen in prestige in the past few decades, there is still a lot of prejudice, and a lot of chauvinism, especially in the church. It tends to show up a lot among evangelical Christians. You just have to decide how you're going to deal with it. Being a ministry wife gives you a platform to model good reactions when people treat you as an appendage to your husband—or ignore you altogether! Use it as an opportunity to show a gracious spirit.

As for me, I try to take all apparent insults as though they are compliments and not let them become personal. Being called "the pastor's wife" or "the missionary's wife" *is* a compliment in one way. It's giving us a title in the sense of something they feel about us. "This is not just any old wife. This is our *minister's* wife." Try not to take it as a putdown. For some people it really is a title of honor. They may not stop to think that you have a name and an identity separate from your husband's. Some of these people have lived in a church culture where *they* may not have had their own identities respected, and they merely see you through that cultural filter.

> You have a name and an identity separate from your husband's. Lovingly insist on being the normal, wonderful person you are.

But there is again the stereotype in people's minds of what the pastor's wife is to be called and behave like, to dress like, to *be* like. You can lovingly break the stereotype by insisting on being the very normal, wonderful person you are. It may take a little bit of confrontation, of saying, "You know, you just said this. It got to me because . . . " They may not have any idea of how labels make you feel. Much of the time they don't intend any harm.

There are labels, and there are opinions, and some of those opinions are strong and carry a lot of weight in the ministry group. I will deal more with the subject of expectations and criticisms in Chapter 8.

For now, try to see what you need to separate from your self-image. And learn to cultivate those things that *should* affect the way you see yourself. Learn to say—every day—"Just because I'm me"—I'm exactly right for my husband and for what God has in mind!

---

*O God, our help in ages past,*
*Our hope for years to come,*
*Our shelter from the stormy blast,*
*And our eternal home.*
*—Isaac Watts*

# ■ For Further Information . . .

*High Call, High Privilege* by Gail MacDonald. Tyndale House Publishers, 1986.
A personal glimpse into the life and struggles of a pastor's wife. Gail shares helpful lessons from life on our functions as a woman, wife, mother, and leader. Not only a good book for the new ministry wife but for the seasoned one as well.

*Secret Passions of the Christian Woman* by Carol Kent. NavPress, 1989.
Carol Kent's honest questions and intriguing insights on dealing with passions and longings in a God-honoring fashion make this a book for every woman. While our deepest passions are known intimately by our Lord, we are not always in touch with them ourselves! This book is a rich encounter with the hidden heartbeat of women today—with the passions that determine our lifestyles, our behaviors, our attitudes, and ultimately, our ability to serve the One who knows us better than we know ourselves. A discussion guide is also available.

*Liberating Ministry from the Success Syndrome* by Kent and Barbara Hughes.
A husband-wife story that shares how to escape the depression and marital stress of living by "numbers." Very encouraging.

# 2

# A Challenge or a Chain?

GOT ANY RIVERS YOU THINK ARE UNCROSSABLE?
GOT ANY MOUNTAINS YOU CAN'T TUNNEL THROUGH?
GOD SPECIALIZES IN THINGS THOUGHT IMPOSSIBLE,
AND HE CAN DO WHAT NO OTHER POWER CAN DO.
—CORRIE TEN BOOM

A seminary student once said to me, "You know, I married a dentist. Then he decided to go into ministry, and that's fine. I'm by his side and I'll go along with him. I've got my own business, my own career, and a move won't disrupt it; I'm going on with that. But he needn't expect me to spend all my spare time in the church. After all, I didn't spend all my spare time in the dentist's office."

I can understand her feelings, but I also know that she and her husband are in for some rough times together. We talked about the one difference between ministry and other vocations, because whether you spend your time in the dentist's or the doctor's or the CPA's office is really irrelevant. Ministry has some elements about it that put it into a category all its own, and if we know about that before we get into it, we can save ourselves a lot of grief.

## The Challenges of Ministry

Ministering to others holds some specific challenges. Two very important considerations are *time* and *emotional energy.*

| Ministry is a night job. | For one thing, ministry is something you do at night. I don't understand how a couple can go all the way through seminary and not have that figured out. But I do know that once you get out of semi- |

nary and into the ministry, stress and problems between couples erupt, often because of the time the wife spends alone in the evenings. I hear it all the time: "He's out every night of the week."

"But what did you expect?" I ask. "After all, you're dealing with volunteers—with lay people. When are they going to be there for your husband? At night. So the very nature of the job requires that there will be a good amount of evening work." You can get very frustrated about that, and the tensions can spill over into bad attitudes toward the church, towards those who are keeping your husband away from you or the family.

Eventually, you will have to temper such demands. I have had young women say, "We need him home at six or seven in the evening to help put the children to bed." Or, "Since he's a pastor, maybe one night or even two nights a week are all right, but absolutely no more." As ministry wives, we need to be very flexible. There are some very practical things that go along with being called into Christian partnership, and one of them is a schedule that has to be regularly reorganized. Priorities will need to be constantly re-evaluated.

Another special challenge to the vocation of ministry is the emotional investment necessary. There is an enormous energy drain as you give to others. Other professionals, such as psychologists, doctors, teachers, and counselors, also have a lot of emotional investment in the people they serve. But most of those professionals go home at night, leaving their clients behind them. There is a separation between work and home for them, however fine the line. I know that some of these good people put in plenty of overtime, and many, in fact, care much more than their professions require, but it is never really "expected" of them to be on call day and night, all hours, indefinitely. In the ministry, it is *expected*. Why? One reason is that the church is a family. Your relationships are more or less permanent. Let me clarify that. As far as God is concerned, the people to whom you have gone to minister to are a permanent part of your life, sort of like your spiritual family members. You never get away from them completely. You can take vacations and put a little distance between you, get away to clear your head and your heart, but until you move away to the next full-time, all-hours, all-days ministry, these people consider themselves closely related to you. In their minds your own family is just part and parcel of the bigger extended group you all belong to.

> God's strength will match any responsibility, however overwhelming it might seem.

Before you get too discouraged over this and decide that ministry is not for you, or that you don't know if you even *like* this family that God has foisted on you, let's remember that God promises you that his strength will always match any responsibility, however overwhelming it might seem. He says, "The one who calls you is faithful and he will do it" (1 Thessalonians 5:24), and he encourages Paul by saying, "My power is made perfect in weakness" (2 Corinthians 12:9-10). Paul adds, "For when I am weak, then I am strong."

God's faithfulness will uphold you in the best and worst times of your ministry. He'll never let you go. Sometimes I think he wants us to feel inadequate so he can show us how steady and strong he is. One of the circumstances he has used most in my life to keep me dependent is "change," and there's always plenty of that in the ministry.

## Change: It's Good, It's Scary!

My husband and I often travel together. As soon as we check into our hotel room I busy myself emptying my suitcase into the hotel furniture.

"What are you doing?" Stuart asks. "We're only here overnight."

"I'm just nesting; then I'll be ready to face the day," I tell him. Some women struggle with an empty nest; I struggle with a mobile one!

> God never calls without equipping.

Change interrupts my nesting habits, intrudes into my comfort zone. Say the word *change*, and I freeze. We ministry wives are subject to huge amounts of the stuff. I have learned to live to the full—wherever I am—by simply pretending I'll be there forever. Otherwise I'd never get involved in a new project, or invest myself in someone's life, or bother to contribute to a group.

Having survived years of frequent change remarkably well, I must admit I have found some benefits. Change can be a tremendous incentive for spiritual growth. Changes bring new life experiences with opportunities to discover and use new personal skills.

Change challenges us. All of us need something to jar us out of our rut—which someone has said "is only a coffin with the ends knocked out!"

With change we have a new start, a clean page, an opportunity to try again. That hope renews us. It's a chance to do it right this time.

Another reason we need to work hard at responding well to change is to model our response to the fellowship, particularly the women's ministry. Women in general and women's groups in particular like to do things as they have always been done. Our favorite text is, "As it was in the beginning, is now and ever shall be, world without end, Amen." I think that more difficult personalities show up in churches when you try to institute change than for any other reason. I heard about a church that terminated their pastor because he tried to change things. The incoming pastor took note of this, and when he wanted to change the piano from the left side of the sanctuary to the right side, wisely decided to move it an inch a month! There was no church split this time! I don't know if there was any truth in that story, but I do know you have to move the piano an inch a month (after all, it's always been there) and not try to do the job in ten minutes. You have to take people at the pace they are willing to go. Again, if we can see that change can change us as we institute it, maybe our example will help when the more corporate changes in the fellowship need to be made.

> Ministry is constant change. Take people at the pace they are willing to go.

Anxiety may be the most difficult aspect of change, but every anxious thought gives an opportunity to trust God in a new way.

Change forces us to evaluate our lives. *Where have I been, where am I now, and where am I going?*

So if we look at ministry as constant change—which, given that people are our business, is pretty much the truth—then we can take a positive, "growth" approach rather than falling back into negative thought patterns.

I have found that nothing wearies me faster than anxiety and the fear of change. In taking the negative approach to change, I work against my own survival.

> *Worry never robs tomorrow of its sorrow, it only saps today of its strength.*—Corrie Ten Boom

There are many days that a ministry wife simply has to decide for survival. You can only be negative for so long before you begin to disintegrate.

You may think that I'm sounding awfully negative to be talking like this about those of us in ministry. But I know a lot of women struggle with the "dread" of what God will require of them in a new situation. Some would say, "Jill, it's not what *God* requires of me that is sapping my strength, but what the *church* thinks that God requires of me." I have known women who were so emotionally burdened by their roles as ministry wives that they did speak in terms of *survival*.

Once you have released yourself of certain burdensome expectations you are not intended to carry, you'll find the energy to accept change and live with it positively. In the following chapters, we will talk about expectations, about burdens to bear or not to bear, and about balance. If what you've read in this chapter so far frightens you, please don't stop here. We have to face the frightening things first. We have to understand what our lives are really about, and what problems are involved in this business of being a ministry wife. I'm saving the best news for later, so don't be discouraged.

> You do not need to carry the burden of expectations.

## Finding a Biblical Model: Peter and His Wife

I looked to the Scriptures, trying to find a couple to use as a model of a healthy ministry partnership, because I love to use examples. But this couple was difficult to find. In Genesis, there's Adam and Eve. But you can't really use them—look at how things turned out in their family! Next you look at Joseph's family and find out that the brothers threw their little brother into a pit. Perhaps a little jealousy and parental favoritism? Better not use that model!

Even when you peruse the New Testament it's difficult to find a couple we can relate to, one we can bring into our twentieth century and say, "Okay, let's see what we can learn." But, peeking around the corner of the verse, which is a habit I have, I found a lady standing in the shadows: Peter's wife.

You're thinking, *Who? Did he have a wife?* Yes, Peter had a wife. And as I studied 1 Peter 3 with this in mind, I realized that he was writing portions of his letter about marriage—perhaps aimed at young couples in the dispersion. Some women had become believers and wanted to know how to influence their men for Christ. Possibly marriage was a real issue for other people married to believers. There were difficulties and problems relating to the dangerous days in which they all lived, and, after all, the views about marriage at that time in the surrounding pagan cultures were not exactly in line with Christianity. Some instruction and explanation were called for.

> The apostle Peter and his wife were committed believers who traveled together.

When he speaks, a pastor usually draws much from his own experience, good or bad. I can't believe that Peter wrote portions of 1 Peter 3 without having himself and his wife in mind. I don't think you can give a talk on marriage partnership without doing that. And so I read 1 Peter 3:1-7 and the relevant verses in chapter 4 with that in mind. Was Peter drawing from his own experience with his wife? It's a guess, but I would think that much of what he said was being put into effect in his own marriage relationship. That gave me a fresh approach to this part of the Scriptures, and I came out of that study having a lot to share with ministry husbands and wives.

So we know that Peter was a disciple of Jesus, and we know that he had a wife. But what kind of a wife? A sideline remark by the apostle Paul gives us the clue that she was also a disciple. Paul, in the face of criticism he was receiving, is defending his position. He's looking at the apostles who are on the road in ministry, and he's saying to his accusers, "I have a right to take a believing wife along with me like Peter and the other apostles do, but I choose not to do it. I waive my right for the sake of the Gospel" (1 Corinthians 9:3-6, paraphrased). This is a clear indication that both Peter and his wife were committed believers who traveled and worked together in the ministry.

> Peter's wife, a gentle Galilean homespun girl, was pulled into the very center of ministry.

We may wonder, *What do Peter and his wife have to do with us? That was a long, long time ago.* But it has everything to do with us, because Peter and his wife were in ministry, and because Peter specifically addresses husbands and wives in his letters. He is a big leader in the church. He was persecuted, jailed, empowered by the Holy Spirit, and used mightily in the spread of the gospel. From the first time he brought home this itinerant preacher named Jesus, whom Peter's wife no doubt fed and whom Peter's wife watched heal her own mother on the spot, we know that this woman was pulled into the very center of ministry.

There's a good chance that Peter's wife was a "ministry widow" for a time, possibly for three years. There's no indication that she traveled with the disciples during Jesus' three years of ministry. Maybe she saw her husband when the group's travels brought them close by. Maybe she followed along when she was able, did her best to keep up with what was happening to her husband. I'm sure those three years were a shock to her, this woman who for years had been a simple fisherman's wife, a gentle Galilean homespun girl.

Modern counterparts can be found in Ruth Tucker's *First Ladies of the Parish: Historical Portraits of Pastors' Wives*, which gives us a fascinating account of wives of famous men like Luther, Calvin, Wesley, and Spurgeon. "So often it was assumed that the multi-talented celebrated pastor should have an equally capable wife" (p. 150). Catherine Marshall wrote, "I could by no means measure up to such a standard" (p. 151). Catherine sought to find her niche. "At only 23 the young girl who had slid up the back stairs to avoid involvement with people now had to be hostess to a steady stream of social functions in one of Washington's largest downtown churches. She quickly discovered that the expectations for that role were far higher than she could fulfill" (p. 150). Someone who is naturally as shy as Catherine was will need to believe in a God who perfectly matches his ministry couples for the task he has in mind.

I'm sure this period of inadequacy and loneliness had not been on Peter's wife's agenda when she married him. But one day Jesus walked into her life and took off with her husband for three years, and she had to adjust to a whole new world.

> God perfectly matches his ministry couples for the task he has in mind.

Maybe she had a brood of children to look after. What happened to her income during those three years I wonder? Did she and the children move back to her parents' home until—as the relatives were sure to say—her husband came to his senses? Did she live with the ridicule of family and neighbors? Can you imagine her uncertainty? Here is a woman who knew the meaning of change and of her world being turned upside-down. Probably the only thing that helped her was the memory of Jesus in her home, healing the hordes of sick at her door, preaching words of encouragement like no one she'd ever heard. Hadn't she seen her own mother instantly cured of the fever? I believe that those memories of Jesus himself—her own forming faith in him—could have been the only thing Peter's wife had to hang onto in those early years. She had the knowledge of Peter's love for her, of course, but even in a strong marriage it's unsettling for the husband to just quit his job and take off. Any wife would feel insecure and question this man she was married to. But she had her own memories of Jesus. She had her own faith in the Son of God.

Throughout the rest of this book, we are going to look at some of the advice Peter gave in his letters. We're going to think about the stresses and strains that come to the life of a ministry couple and particularly a ministry wife. And we'll discuss some practical ways that you can deal with the negatives and emphasize the positives.

> **Peter's wife was one of the pioneers.**

If you have picked up this book because you are hurting, wondering what to do in your situation, remember Peter's wife. She was one of the pioneers. She lived with pain and loneliness and uncertainty. But she had her own relationship with Jesus. And so do you.

---

*Drink deep and full of the love of God, and the love of wife and child, of husband and friend, will grow holier and healthier and simpler and grander.—Oswald Chambers*

---

# ■ For Further Information . . .

*From Jerusalem to Irian Jaya: A Biographical History of Christian Missions* by Ruth A. Tucker. Zondervan, 1983.
A book on women pioneers.

*When Your Husband Is Part of a Staff.* Pamphlet by Marilyn Hansen, Called Together Ministries, 20820 Avis Avenue, Torrance, CA 90503.
For the associate pastor's wife. Deals with how the associate or youth minister's wife (or wives of other church staff members) experiences church life differently from the wife of the senior pastor. This booklet will help you handle the special pressures and relationships involved in this unique role.

# 3

# Christ as Governor—Not Guest

WE ARE ALL DANGEROUS FOLK
WITHOUT GOD'S CONTROLLING HAND.
—*WILLIAM WARD AYER*

THE PULPIT IS A DANGEROUS PLACE
FOR ANY SON OF ADAM.
—*JOHN STOTT*

I would add to John Stott's quote that the parsonage is a dangerous place for any daughter of Eve. Eve used or rather abused her opportunity to partner Adam in their God-given situation, to opt out of obedience and submission to the sovereign will of God. I have discovered that Eve lives in me. There is always that "pull" to be my own goddess and do my own thing instead of the thing God has called me to do. The ministry affords a wife both the chance to run herself ragged or to opt out of all responsibilities and put herself and her family first. Some ministry wives I meet were far more involved in the church as lay wives than they are now as full-time ministry wives.

I often ask them the question, "What would you be doing if you weren't married to the pastor? Or, what would you be doing in this church if you were married to a layman? If you think of yourself as belonging to this body of believers as a committed disciple, what do you think you should be doing?"

> Your personal relationship with Christ should take an upturn when you get married.

I ask this question because I believe that we shouldn't necessarily stop what we're doing and being because we get married, or at least we shouldn't if we are believers. Peter talks about being heirs together of the gracious gift of eternal life (1 Peter 3:7). And in another part of the Scriptures we learn that we are personal heirs with Christ. Our personal relationship with Christ should not take a downturn if we get married; it should take an upturn. In other words, we go on with the Lord.

Yes, you become one with your husband, and you have this incredible privilege of being married to a man whom God has chosen in a very special way to do a very special job, but that does not negate you. You do not become a non-person, somebody whose own abilities and personality have disappeared. Hopefully you are becoming more like Christ every day. As a Christian wife, that should be your primary goal, whether or not you're married to a church leader. I believe that Peter and his wife emphasized that goal of becoming more Christlike and doing it together. They were heirs together of the gracious gift of eternal life (see 1 Peter 3).

Unfortunately, many women don't see themselves in this way. They have allowed their lives—their gifts and God's plan for them—to be swallowed up in their new identity, even using it to get them out of all service. Often when I organize ministry wives' conferences, we place the women in small groups and discuss these issues together. Usually over half the wives in the group object to the statement about being "heirs together." They say to me, "What do you mean when you say that I'm called? Yes, I'm a Christian, but I'll stand on the sidelines and be the cheerleader. I'll be a supportive spouse, but I'm not called. *He's* called. They didn't hire me; they hired him."

"True," I reply, "but I trust he went to the place he serves because he believed God had 'called' him to serve him there and not because a group of people hired him. What is a call? If you are a disciple then you're *called to follow him in service, too,* alongside your husband."

"Well, yes," the answer comes, "but I'm not called like my husband is."

"No, but you're called like you are!"

What I mean by "called" is the sense of personal spiritual responsibility each of us has before God. It is our responsibility to serve in discipleship.

In the role and function where you find yourself, your calling has to be worked out. But you most definitely *are* called to serve or minister, if you claim to be a disciple of Jesus. You are a disciple disguised as a ministry wife, just as somebody else might be a disciple disguised as a machine operator or as a grade-school teacher. The things that we do, the tasks we perform are secondary to who we are in Christ.

> You are a disciple of Jesus disguised as a ministry wife.

---

*What we love we shall grow to resemble.*
—Bernard of Clairvaux

---

## Who Is Jesus to You?

There is a story in John 2 about Jesus going to the wedding in Cana. You know the story—he was invited as a guest, and he went graciously and sat beside all the other guests. As custom would have it, the governor ("master," in NIV) of the feast sat between the bride and groom at the head table. He was in charge of the wedding; he gave the orders.

During the feast, a serious thing happened—the wine ran out. Instead of going to the governor (who they should have gone to) the servants went to Mary. They said, "The wine's run out." It doesn't say *why* they went to Mary. Maybe they went to her because she was in charge of the food and the wine—I don't know. They didn't know what they were going to do. It would have been a disgrace in that culture to run out of food or drink. They certainly didn't look to Jesus for a miracle because he hadn't done any yet. But still, when Mary told them to, they approached Jesus and told him, "The wine's run out."

Jesus said, "Fill the jars with water . . . Now draw some out and take it to the master of the banquet" (John 2:7-8). And the servants obeyed, even though they were risking their jobs by doing what he told them to do. As far as they knew they believed they would be serving water, but they poured the drink anyway—and the miracle happened. The governor was very surprised and exclaimed, "This wine is better than any we've had before!" In fact, he said, "Everyone brings out the choice wine first and then the cheaper wine after the guests have had too much to drink; But you have saved the best till now" (John 2:10).

Jesus turned the water into wine when he took over and gave the orders.

> Is Christ the governor of your marriage?

Let's take that story and use it as a picture of marriage for a minute. So many people I know *want Jesus as a guest at their wedding, but they do not want him as the governor of their marriage.* And I believe that both spouses, especially in ministry, have to make sure that Jesus is the governor of their marriage. First he must be governor of their lives individually. How do you know if he's the governor? As Mary said to the servants in the story, "Do whatever he tells you" (John 2:5). What about you? Are you doing what he's telling you to do? Are you being obedient? Is he governor?

When Jesus quit being the guest in that marriage, that wedding, and became the governor, he turned the water into wine and the Bible tells us it was better than anything they'd had before. In the same way, I believe a ministry partnership can be incredibly exciting, better than anything that has gone before. He, as the Scripture says, "has saved the best wine until now." All the problems that show up

> God has saved the best for you till now.

on surveys do not need to be if the principle of Christian partnership is right, if God is the God of your individual life, and if God is the governor of your relationship with your husband.

> *A good marriage is not*
> *a contract between two persons*
> *but a sacred covenant between three.*
> *Too often Christ is never invited*
> *to the wedding and finds no room*
> *in the home.—Donald T. Kauffman*

### The Meaning of Commitment

When Stuart and I got engaged, we wanted a ring with three diamonds, not only because that was typical then of the European engagement ring, but also because it was a symbol for us. We thought of Christ as the middle stone and Stuart and I on either side. Every day as my eye catches my engagement ring I am reminded of all that it stands for. It tells me once more that God is the governor of our marriage. And that facet of life together is something I have had cause to remember, especially as a ministry wife.

I have learned it is not necessarily each partner's full commitment to God and each other that makes it work—but God's commitment to us. He is the third strand. He is totally given to making all of this work. We may fade or renege, but he remains faithful.

> *A cord of three strands is not quickly broken.*—Ecclesiastes 4:12

Therefore God must be at the center of our partnership. We must bank on his involvement. He is "for" us. Then we need to operate under the assumption that we, too, are as committed to ministry as our husbands are. If not, we are going to have a miserable time in full-time service. It is from this source of commitment—his and ours—that we get the excitement and joy that accompany fruitful ministry.

Joshua said, "As for me and my house, *we* will serve the Lord" (Joshua 24:15). It starts with "me": as for *me*, I'm going to serve the Lord. Then my husband and I together will serve him. And the children, too, who are not going to be standing on the sidelines but, rather, doing their own part to be in this together—the Lord, my husband, me, and the kids. This "family focus" lends to harmony in the home.

**When Christ is first, the faces of all your struggles change.**

Far too many partnerships are not harmonious precisely because many wives have no sense of purpose or worth and feel they are being dragged along on the tails of their husbands' "call." As a believer, your calling is assured. If you are married, then God intends that you unravel the mysteries of all this together:

listening intently to one another, praying together, learning and being obedient together.

It's important to know within yourself where Jesus is in your life. That is the real issue. When Christ is first, the faces of all your other struggles change. For one thing, they are placed squarely in his care. You no longer have to deal with them on your own. You have a heavenly Partner.

---

*Build your hope on Jesus Christ.*
*No matter if there are a hundred and one things*
*that press, resolutely exclude them all*
*and look to God.*—Mrs. Charles E. Cowman

---

# ■ For Further Information . . .

"Our Favorite Verse," the personal testimony of Stuart and Jill Briscoe. For further information, write to: Briscoe Ministries, Elmbrook Church, 777 South Barker Rd., Waukesha, WI 53186.

# 4

# How Open Is Open?

If we are going to be in ministry, we're going to have to learn that our marriage is not our marriage. Our home is not our home. Our parsonage is not our parsonage (and I don't mean it belongs to the church). It all belongs to the Lord.

These are hard sayings, but if you are a ministry wife, you have already discovered them to be true. Most of us learn the hard way.

## Becoming a Receiver

Years ago, shortly after I had become a Christian, I read a book, written by a missionary, called *Have We No Rights?* I'm so glad I read it early in my walk with the Lord. It was a wonderful treasure, written by a veteran missionary. When she went to the field she assumed she had rights—the right to privacy in her own home, the right to eat the way she wanted to, with the implements she chose, the right to do all sorts of things she had always done. But God began to deal with her until she came to the point of saying, "I have no rights." And what a difference that made for her!

This really impressed me deeply because I'm English, and the Englishman's home is his castle. If you struggle with privacy problems in the ministry, I really understand—because born into me is my English lady's sense of privacy. I don't "naturally" respond well to the "intrusion" that is part and parcel of serving the Lord. And so for me to learn how to receive people in Jesus' name, at any time of the day or night, has been difficult.

> Our homes belong to Jesus, and he has every right to invite anyone he likes into them!

If our homes belong to him, Jesus has every right to invite anyone he likes into them! And Jesus has some weird friends. I began to note right away that Jesus' friends were not always the sort of people I would have thought of inviting in for an evening, and I certainly didn't want some of them sleeping in our beds or staying very long, and I didn't want to feed them more than one meal unless I had to. Above all, I wasn't sure I wanted them mixing with our children!

Learning what it meant to be a receiver—to be hospitable—turned my life upside down.

As Peter followed Jesus he began to receive all sorts of people into his life—a leper, a paralyzed man, and outcasts of every sort. When you realize that Peter was a true-blue Jew, you can understand how much he must have struggled with this. Jews weren't supposed to eat with "unclean" (Gentile) or deformed folk. They weren't supposed to go anywhere near dead bodies, either. Jesus was busy meeting with the unclean, healing the deformed, and touching dead bodies. He was even handling lepers! Jewish Peter suffered a set of traumatic spiritual and social shocks. Jesus was teaching him a hard lesson. "Peter," he was saying, "if you are a disciple of mine, you're going to have to receive the world. The people you call common or unclean you are going to have to learn to love, because I made them. I'm going to die for them. That's all part of following me. These are my people. This is my family. This is how it's going to be."

I believe a strong principle of Christian partnership is that both husband and wife have to work at being receivers. This is harder for some than for others. Let's examine this area we call "hospitality."

## Hospitality and Hostessing

In Scripture hospitality is not a gift but a command. And, incidentally, it didn't have much to do with women in the beginning. In 1 Timothy 3:2 and Titus 1:8 it is the men who are commanded to be hospitable; the word actually means "the love of strangers." Strangers would often come into the local church or assembly, as it was called, and as they did, a leader would make a beeline for them and take them home to "the little woman," who hopefully had the gift of hostessing. Hospitality involves hostessing: what you do with the people who come into your home.

> Hospitality is not a gift— it's a command.

Hostessing, that lovely gift that you might or might not possess, is the ability to make the environment such that the stranger feels welcome—to make it comfortable, to make it pleasant, to make it as pretty as you can with what you've got. The idea is to make it a place people want to come to. That's the gift of hostessing, and you know as well as I do that some people have it and some people don't. I do not have it in large measure, so what I do is to make friends with someone who does! And these "hostess friends" teach me the ropes. You can only learn so much—as hostessing really is a talent. But you can develop and improve the hostess skills you do have.

In Mark 1:29, when Jesus left the synagogue with James and John to go to the home of Simon and Andrew, Simon's mother-in-law was in bed with a fever, and they told Jesus about it. Perhaps this is when Peter's wife met Christ for the first time. Jesus touched the mother-in-law, the fever left her, and she began to wait on them. That evening after sunset the people brought all the sick and all the demon-possessed to Peter's house. In fact, "the whole town gathered at the door" (Mark 1:33).

> You can develop and improve the hostess skills you do have.

I have that phrase underlined: *The whole town gathered at the door.* Do you ever feel as if that is happening to you? You can't be in ministry very long before you get this awful feeling—*Why does it have to be our door?* But if you're doing your job, the world will be beating a path to your door. Do you know why? Because if they know that Jesus is in the house, they'll be there. You see, they're not coming to see your drapes or to taste your food. They're coming because they know Jesus is in residence.

Just a bit later in the Gospel of Mark four desperate men, carrying a crippled friend, tear up the roof to get to Jesus (Mark 2:4). Would you have liked for that to have been *your* house? The friends who brought the crippled man didn't care about the owner—his house or his furniture! All they knew was that Jesus was in there, and they were determined to get help for their friend. In the same way, a hurting, needy world will often disregard you and your property when they're aware that Christ is present.

When the whole town is gathered at your door, what do you do, human that you are? I have found out that I just cope. When I get to heaven I want to ask Peter's wife a lot of questions. How did she cope? I want to ask her if she had the gift of hostessing. The Bible doesn't really tell me, and that frustrates me. Was she an introvert or an extrovert? Did it drain her to be surrounded by people or did she thrive on it? Some people do thrive on all this activity. Being around others energizes them. They run down in solitude.

I wonder about Peter's wife, whose home became a meeting place for the masses. What I really think is that it didn't matter if she had the gift of hostessing or not. It didn't matter what her personality type was either, because when the world is at your door, you simply do it. You put the kettle on. If a loaf of bread is all you have in the house, you make toast.

> Did Peter's wife have the gift of hostessing?

Those of you in youth work who have teenagers running all over your house know what I'm talking about. The last nice thing we had in our home, a beautiful glass bowl, went flying while we had a house full of teenagers. I thought *Oh no!* And then the Lord said, *Good. That's the last good thing you have that you could worry about. Now you don't even need to go through this awful "Oh no, there goes my glass bowl" again.* But it was hard. Those kids wore through our carpets and scraped our furniture and, I suspect, slipped one or two little trinkets into their pockets! We were in youth work in Europe for fourteen years—working with kids, many of them from the street. You can't do that kind of work without having the teenagers themselves in your home. Maybe adult work is a little different, but if you work with youth they *will* need to be in your home. This doesn't mean you shouldn't attempt to corral them. I remember putting a big sign on the bottom of the stairs that said, "Where do you think you're going?" It didn't stop them from spreading all over the house, but at least it was an attempt—it made *me* feel better. This is part of what it means to love strangers.

But we have to remember that it's not *us* loving the strangers. It's Jesus, who is living in us. In 1 Timothy 5:10 the women are commanded to be hospitable as well as the men. For us it is a task that comes in the context of ministry partnership.

This might mean that your husband has to put on an apron sometimes, too, to reverse cultural roles. His part might not be just to bring hordes of people home for you to cope with. His part has to be: "Now how can we do this together?" For some men that's difficult because they have come from very strict male/female role-oriented backgrounds. Although men are much more acclimated to sharing housework these days—much more than in my early married years— some men still don't think of helping in the home. They assume that is the wife's role. If this is a problem area in your marriage, you should gently point out the need for help before you get to a point of resentment. In 1 Peter 5:5-6, Peter says, "Clothe yourselves with humility toward one another because 'God opposes the proud but gives grace to the humble.' Humble yourselves, therefore . . .'" When Peter suggested we "tie humility round us like a towel" I'm sure he was remembering Jesus stripping to the waist, girding himself with a towel, and doing women's work—as he washed Peter's feet. If we are going to be able to accomplish the work of hospitality, our menfolk will need to do some part of our "women's work" for us or with us.

> Loving strangers is part of what it means to love Jesus.

---

*If we want to touch people, we have to get out of our shell and take some risks.*—Ruth Senter

---

## The Meaning of Availability

One Christmas, when we had been in the States about a year, Stuart came walking in, dressed in his suit, tying his tie, and I said to him, "What are you doing?"

"Oh, I have a wedding," he replied.

"A *what*? On Christmas Day?" I managed to stutter.

"Well, I'm sorry I forgot to tell you," he said. "And one more thing—it's here."

Now, I could have asked a lot of questions. I could have asked "Why?" in anger. But I managed not to. Instead I asked, "When?"

And he said, "In about half an hour."

Here I was on Christmas Day, cooking dinner, the three kids creating happy chaos in the living room, Christmas wrapping and just-opened gifts all over the floor. Of course, since it was Christmas Day, I hadn't bothered to do my hair or dress up— just a relaxed day at home with the family, right? But there was no time even to get mad! I rounded up the children, and we set about tidying the place in less than half an hour. Stuart "put an apron on" and helped, too. Forget the chaos, or that the smell of roasting turkey was wafting through every room of the house and the kitchen was a mess; we were going to have a wedding.

Stuart explained then that it was a situation where the parents wouldn't come to the wedding. It was a tough time for that young couple. So we did the best we could. In the middle of the ceremony, there was a knock at the door and one set of parents arrived in tears. They had decided that they should be at the wedding after all. But there were two sets of parents, and the other set arrived ten minutes later! They were ready to kill each other—but ended up making the wedding as happy as possible for their children.

Such things sometimes happen. And when they do, we need to say to ourselves, "This is probably never going to happen again." It probably will only happen once; there are a lot of things that only happen once. The sad thing is that I've seen marriages almost split over that one incident. But if you know that these sorts of

> There are a lot of things that only happen once. Remembering that simple fact will help us live through them.

things usually won't happen again, that helps you get through them when they do.

So as soon as such a situation begins, and you think, *Is this a nightmare? I can't believe it's happening,* tell yourself, *Well, it's only going to happen once.* That kind of thinking is a real key to surviving God's many surprises that come the way of the ministry couple.

I remember trying to mail a letter once. It was during the Christmas season. The situation was very frustrating. Every time I went to the post office, it was closed. Suddenly this idea came into my head. As a believer, as a ministry wife, I realized I had no right to have hours "like the post office." That revelation from years ago has helped me tremendously. Every time I go past a post office I think about that. And I thought about it on the day of that wedding. As ministry wives and husbands, we don't have a right to have hours like the post office, even on Christmas Day!

> As believers, we have no right to have hours like the post office.

---

> *Gifts can be **an** evidence of the fullness of the Holy Spirit. Fruit is **the** evidence.*—Anonymous

---

## People Matter More than Schedules

I have to work at availability because I'm a scheduled sort of person. Efficiency is one of my gifts. But sometimes, with my personality type, it is very hard to be flexible. Over the years I've constantly had to remind myself that people matter more than schedules.

We see this in the life of Jesus. He had just heard about John the Baptist's death, and he was devastated. John was a dear friend—actually, one of Jesus' relatives. Somebody that Jesus loved very much had just been brutally murdered, his severed head displayed on a plate at a wild party.

When Jesus was told about it, he decided that he needed to get away for a while. It's hard to bear private grief publicly. He and the disciples had been working hard—they were exhausted. They had needed a break even before this awful shock. So Jesus says, "Come on. Let's get away. Let's go to the other side of the lake." Desperately exhausted, weary in welldoing, they get into the boat, looking forward to their mini-vacation, and what happens? The people see where they're going, and five thousand plus of them make the trip around the water and meet them as they land! Can't you imagine whoever's rowing saying, "Oh no. Should we turn around, Master, and go back the other way? They'll never have the strength to run all the way around again."

And Jesus says, "No. They needn't go away. We'll feed them." Now that's availability! And what does he do? He feeds five thousand men—not counting the women and children.

> How can you cope when you end up with minimum time away when you've planned on much, much more?

And then Jesus does what he originally intended to do. Climbs the mountain and spends time with God. Jesus got his minimum time alone when he was looking for maximum time. That happens in ministry—you end up with minimum time away when you had planned on much, much more. It happened to Jesus, and it will happen to us, also.

There will be times in ministry when you arrive somewhere for a much needed break, and you will be met by what feels like five thousand people, all demanding your attention. The Bible says that Jesus was moved with compassion when he saw the multitudes and was able to put aside his own personal problems in order to meet others' needs. Jesus believed that people mattered more than his own personal plans.

In a way, Jesus led a planless life. Not a purposeless life, but a planless one. He allowed his heavenly Father to change his schedule as he wished. He probably did have something in mind each day about what he planned to do. Perhaps he wanted to go from Jerusalem to Jericho on a ministry tour. Maybe he hoped to spend time with family or friends. Perhaps he planned to retreat for a day of prayer with his disciples. But when he was interrupted by the multitude he responded to the needs of those people. He didn't slam the door in their faces or react in anger or resentment.

> Jesus led a planless life, but not a purposeless one.

---

*Oh, to have one's soul as a field under heavenly cultivation, no wilderness but a garden of the Lord, walled around with grace, planted with instruction, visited by love, weeded by heavenly discipline, guarded by divine power. One's soul thus favored is prepared to yield fruit unto the glory of God.*—Charles Spurgeon

---

## Learning to Cope

When we were serving in a youth mission, I had a leader's wife who was a wonderful model of availability for me. She taught me more in this regard than anybody else I've ever met. Working with hundreds of teenagers from all over the world was very much an on-the-go type of ministry. We lived right there among them; we could seldom get away.

I would be trailing along behind Joan, trying to ask her an important question, and she would be going from the bread pantry to the dining room or from the office to the bedroom, and she'd just say, "Come on. Come with me. Ask me while I'm going." I learned from her to take people with me and that I don't have to stop whatever I'm doing if someone wants to ask me questions. When the kids would come over, for example, I learned to say, "Well, if you don't mind sitting here as I do this ironing, I'll be happy to chat with you." You do what you need to do and deal with people in the middle of it all. You let the people "be" there, but you don't have to drop everything you're doing. In fact, sometimes you *can't* just stop a project if you're busy and have children and a home to keep in some semblance of order.

I used to watch Joan as she was stopped time and time again between point A and point B. At times I would get impatient because I knew how important it was for her to get to the office or the bedroom or the pantry or wherever she was going. But she would stop and move that person who had met her with a question to the top of her priority list. You would have thought there was no one in the world but that girl or boy who needed her attention at that moment. One time I said to her, "Joan, I am so uptight it's driving me crazy. Can't you just tell them to come back later? Can't you just walk past them and do what I know you need to do?"

> Availability doesn't mean you have to drop everything you're doing to "be there" for someone.

And she said, "Jill, when you are stopped by a multitude of needs you must stop and say, 'This person is center stage in my thinking.' I have learned that if those people are placed there in my life, they are God's blessed interruptions." So from then on I tried to do what she was doing. Sometimes when I was interrupted by the multitude I would even say to the person, "All right. What do you want? Did you know that you're God's blessed interruption?" I got some surprised looks; it may have not been the best application I've made of a lesson, but after a while I did understand more fully how to incorporate Joan's attitude!

Be hospitable, available, flexible. Be like the earthquake-proofed houses in San Francisco: built on the rock but with flexibility in every joint. Then when the upheaval comes, you won't collapse but stand firm.

> Be hospitable, available, and flexible for God's blessed interruptions.

You can't be in ministry long before these conflicts come up (I wasn't). These conflicts between your schedule and the needs of people around you will be part of every day of the rest of your life. Possibly you've been fighting this, especially if you're a "scheduled" person like me. Remember that all you give up is the bondage to your calendar—the hour-by-hour schedule that can become a real taskmaster. Let priorities work themselves out in God's scheme of things every day.

Let me tell you one more story. When all our kids were in college, I worked three months to get us all together for a brief two days over Easter vacation. I planned those two days like I planned little else.

About two weeks before our precious time together I got a letter from a missionary friend. As I opened it I had a sense of foreboding. The letter read:

*Dear Jill and Stuart,*
*I know the sort of home you keep and remembered your kind offer of hospitality, and that's why I have no hesitation asking this favor. My daughter, who's in the States for college, has nowhere to go for Easter, and I took it upon myself to invite her to your home.*

*I know you always have a full house at Easter, so I knew that one
more wouldn't make any difference. Thanks in advance.*

*Lord, it's not fair!* my heart cried out. From experience I
knew it wouldn't be just one college girl; it would be two
other roommates who didn't have anywhere to go either. (Actually it ended up being six!) So I began my bargaining
process with God. I really felt I was grieving a death—the loss
of this special two days with our family—because I knew they
wouldn't be *our* days anymore. So I bargained with God and
said, *Well, God. I'll have her for the whole summer. Will that do? Or
for two whole weeks next semester.* Then, with a final, desperate
offer, I added, *I'll adopt her!* Of course there was no response to
that, and after a while I put the letter on my bed and knelt
down in front of it and prayed, *Lord, I wanted so much for this to
be our time, as a family, and you know that the rest of my life's
always been full of everyone else's children, so I just feel this isn't fair
of you.* When no lightning bolt struck from heaven and I didn't
hear his voice saying, *Okay! You don't have to take them this time!*
the best response I could come up with was, *Well then, Lord, I'll
do it, but don't ever let them know I didn't
want them.* I know that's not very spiritual,
but it was the best I could do. My heart
was still heavy.

An important principle in ministry is:
Don't wait until you can say, "I'm so
thrilled they're coming. Praise the Lord
you've messed up my holiday! God bless
you." You're never going to get to that
point as far as I can see, and if you do,
drop me a line—I'd love to hear from you!

> God
> accepts us
> the way
> we are, not
> the way
> we know
> we should
> be.

I've learned just to tell God what I can do, not what I can't. He
accepts us the way we are, not the way we know we should
be.

And so that's what he did with me. He took me where I
was, and the girls never knew I didn't want them there.

Everyone except me had a wonderful Easter, though not the Easter I had planned.

Years later my daughter and I wrote a book together about our relationship. We sat side by side at the kitchen table, and I said to Judy, "You write about 'this or that' and I'll write about it, too, from my different perspective, and then we'll swap papers." And that's how we wrote that book. At one point we wrote about our open home. We scribbled away and then exchanged papers.

To my amazement she wrote about that Easter, that very incident. What I did not know was that she had been on the edge of all sorts of problems at that time, and it was one of those girls who I had not wanted there who saw it. *I* didn't see it. But this girl whisked my daughter away from the crowd into an empty room and sat her down, and they dealt with it.

We had entertained angels unaware. I sat at the kitchen table that day with Judy and cried. I was able to share with her my struggles that Easter. Later we shared our thoughts verbally with God. Judy prayed, *I'm thankful, Lord, that it turned out that way because I don't know where I'd be if that girl hadn't helped me.* Now Judy is married and offers hospitality to her own "multitude" of needy people.

Although the stories don't always turn out like that, I have many, many experiences I could share of the angels that God has brought to our home in human form. You see, you may be a ministry wife, but God never forgets that you and your family need ministering *to* as well. We think that we spend our lives serving others, but the Lord has a twofold plan. He wants us to learn how to serve others and become more like him. And then he turns around our serving and our situations to heal us, to care for us, and to grow us up, often through the very people we have helped!

> God never forgets that you and your family need someone to minister to you.

Heavenly Father,

Thank you for the privilege of being a ministry wife. Yes, there are a lot of pressures. Yes, there are a lot of stresses. Sometimes you have to discipline me. But above it and beyond it all you remind me that my calling is a privilege. And it's you who thought so highly of me that you've chosen me to be a ministry wife. I pray that you would come to me yourself and point out the Scriptures that will mend and heal, encourage and build, and make me strong so that I can be a force to be reckoned with where the devil is concerned.

In your precious name,

Amen.

# ■ For Further Information . . .

*Creative Hospitality* by Marlene D. LeFever. Tyndale House Publishers, 1980.
A fresh, helpful guide to purposeful entertaining for the entire church family. Packed with out-of-the-ordinary ideas to get you thinking, inviting, and ministering to your church family in a creative way. Will help you assist your church family in having fun together. An excellent gift idea.

*Open Heart, Open Home* by Karen Mains. David C. Cook Publishing Co., 1976.
A wonderful book on hospitality. Tips for finding joy through sharing your home with others.

*The Personal Touch: Encouraging Others through Hospitality* by Rachael Crabb with Raeann Hart. NavPress, 1990.
Encouraging others through hospitality is what this book is all about. You don't need a flair for entertaining. The key is to focus on people, not on preparations. So if you've always wanted to be one of those people who is "natural" at hospitality, you don't need to wait any longer. *The Personal Touch* will give you the ideas and the confidence to practice encouragement with your own unique style.

# 5

# Oh, I Never Expected This!

WE HAVE TO GO THROUGH MANY EXPERIENCES
IN ORDER TO GET THE SPIRITUAL VISION
WHICH IS NEEDED TO SEE THE DIVINE PLAN.
A FILM IS DEVELOPED IN A DARK ROOM.
—ANONYMOUS

Early in our marriage, Stuart and I had some hard choices to make. Two missions wanted us to leave the business world and commit ourselves to full-time ministry. We needed to choose between them—a long and difficult process. We said "no" to one of them because they wanted Stuart to travel. We wanted to be together and didn't want to get involved with an organization that would have Stuart "on the road." So we chose one where he would be the treasurer of the fellowship and be able to stay home. This way we could do the work together that God had brought us together to do.

Within a short time Stuart was on the road, and I was sitting at home saying, "Oh, I never expected this!"

> *Wheresoever a man seeketh his own, there he falleth from love.*—Thomas á Kempis

## Dashed Expectations

If I hear one thing above all else from ministry wives it's that very phrase: "I never expected this!" I can't count the numerous times I've heard such things as, "When I signed up for missions I did not have this in mind." Many ministry wives get where they're going, and then look around and say, "You mean *this* is what we left the business world for?" Or, "*This* is what all those years in seminary have led to?"

When men enter the ministry after having had "secular" careers, they bring a lot of positives to their work. They can bring their educational expertise or vocational experience with them. But I am often faced with the wives of these men who say something like, "Hey, I married a CPA. I didn't marry a Christian-education director." A pastor's wife said to me not long ago, "I'm married to a man I didn't marry. I did not marry a pastor, and if I'd known this is what he was going to do, I wouldn't have married him at all," and she meant it! So in some cases there are deep, deep conflicts that are not easily resolved, exacerbated by unfulfilled expectations, the other side of the move into ministry.

> Somehow we can enter the world of "ministry" in rose-colored spectacles.

Add to this the frustrations of a spouse who has been working with lots of resources he doesn't have available to him anymore. I know Stuart struggled with adapting to a very different world from that of a top bank executive when he tried to reorganize the mission offices and finances. He badly wanted to use his knowledge gained from the working world, but he discovered that many mission organizations don't have access to needed resources. The money is not there to hire more staff and update the equipment—or even to possess the equipment necessary to do the job! Somehow we can enter the world of "ministry" in rose-colored spectacles—never expecting the standard of operation to be as low as we find it. Then our menfolk have to work at a level well below their training or capacity.

We need to pull together at this point, giving each other a sympathetic hearing but encouraging each other with love and Scripture and above all cheerfulness. What Stuart and I learned during that time was that people are God's most precious resources. In the middle of my dashed expectations I needed "people" to fill the lonely hours that my husband was away, while Stuart had to remind himself that we were in the right place, even if the equipment was lacking. God wasn't limited by the absence of a computer!

## God's Resources

We need to be careful that our sense of value isn't determined by our resources, the numbers that turn up to worship (as we discussed in an earlier chapter), or the amount of the offerings given on the Lord's Day. It's hard to learn that lesson. Many of us feel we have been working hard at getting nowhere, that our wheels are spinning and, to make matters worse, everybody we meet who goes to another church tells us of innovative programs, special speakers, huge successful events, and a budget that has been met without mentioning money! It's discouraging when the church across the street is getting larger while we are getting smaller, and our slide projector keeps breaking down while the new fellowship on the block uses multi-media on three screens every week. It's hard not to fall into the trap of "comparing"

> Many of us feel we have been working hard at getting nowhere.

or simply giving up. "If only we had more money, overhead
projectors, and wireless microphones," we lament. But the
latest gadgets aren't everything.

While traveling in Africa and visiting missionaries, I noted
with amusement a poster with the words,

> We the unwilling
> led by the unknowing
> are doing the impossible
> for the ungrateful.
> We have done so much
> for so long with so little,
> we are now qualified
> to do anything
> with nothing!

I wonder if you can relate to that? Yet the greatest resource
God has is people, and people have the Holy Spirit. Other
priceless helps for us mortals are prayer, fellowship, the
promises of God from the Word of God, and faith. Add all that
to a person, and you have some pure spiritual resources to
draw on that can empower you to do anything that needs
doing. How do we know? Jesus said so. He said that with faith
(not earth movers) we could move moun-
tains. Paul said so, too. He even went so
far as to say, "When I am weak then I am
strong!" What's more, our "nothingness"
gives God a chance to fill us with his
"somethingness" and blow the devil
away! Little is much when God is in it.

**With faith we can move mountains.**

A great deal can be done for the kingdom by "little servants" with "little skill" and "little training" if they have big
hearts for God. Proverbs 30:24-28 tells us about four small
things God created that made up for their size by their wisdom. The ants have "little" strength, yet they use what they
have to provide for their families. The coneys have "little"

power, but they use the little they have to protect their homes. The locusts have no great leader, but they have fellowship with like-minded locusts and find that there is power in numbers. And the lizard is small enough to be held in the hand, but that gives it grand ideas of possessing the high ground. In other words, little is big if God is in it! You, like me, may sometimes feel like an ant, coney, locust, or lizard, or any other small and rather ridiculous creature. But each of us has, like all of God's live created beings, capabilities far beyond our physical means or size. "If any of you lacks wisdom, he should ask God, who gives generously to all without finding fault, and it will be given to him" (James 1:5). God is God and I am me, but God and me together means that he is well able to work his wonders through me.

> A great deal can be done for the kingdom by "little servants" with "little skill" and "little train- ing" if they have big hearts for God.

This is not to say that resources are not gifts, tools, and means to an end and should all be used, if available, to further kingdom work. I must confess, however, that I have found myself far more nervous when I have had to rely on complicated computers for sound and light presentations, fine-tuned microphones, and intricate and complicated production panels when presenting a musical drama to thousands of people (as has been my experience), than when in the past I have had to stand up in front of masses of wild street kids without any means of amplification at all. I well remember, while engaged in street evangelism, being searingly conscious of the need for God's provision, protection, and power. I had no help then but the power of the Spirit, the Word of God, and the fellowship of a tiny "scared-to-death" team of helpers, whose saving faith was one great burning desire to reach for the stars and tell that mob about the One who made them. Sometimes I yearn for and miss the thrill of that latter experience while thoroughly enjoying and utilizing to the full the former.

Let's thank God for whatever "helps" that, in the economy of God, have been permitted to us, refuse to allow lack of material resources to frustrate us or dampen our spirits, and remember that "people" are God's most precious resources. So whether with a combine harvester or the "old fashioned way" with rakes and pitchforks, let's bring in the harvest!

> **People are God's best resource.**

---

*It is love that asks, that seeks, that knocks, that finds, and that is faithful to what it finds.*—St. Augustine

---

## Following God's Will

Frankly, I have felt desperately inadequate to perform most of the things in ministry that God has set up for me. Being more or less a single parent with my husband continually on the road was one of those things.

When I would want us to look for an easier place to serve, Stuart would say to me, "Jill, we know we must stay here until God leads us out as surely as he led us in." And he was right. We looked back at our guidance and couldn't see how we would have chosen differently, given the information we had at the time. God knew ahead of time what was coming and yet he still led us in that direction. It comes down to God's love and his sovereignty. Either he is leading us in a loving way or he's not. Sometimes knowing that you did follow God's command is the only comfort that can be had when you find yourself in an unexpectedly difficult situation.

So look back if you have any doubts. Check on your guidance. Are you in the place of his appointment? At times that will be just about all the ground you have to stand on—that assurance. He shows us the past. Remember that: we can look back and see his working.

I have come to look at following God's will in this way. Once I sense the direction that God is leading, I need to have a personal Gethsemane, a personal Calvary, and a personal Pentecost.

*The Gethsemane*—pulling myself alongside the will of God when I don't *want* to do that thing. My prayer then becomes—like his—"Not my will but Thine be done" and "I must be about my Father's business."

*The Calvary*—dying to what I would really like to do. This is where the "I" gets crucified with Christ. Remember all those personal rights we thought we had? The availability required of us? The little deaths we suffer as our homes become Grand Central Station? Those are chances to "die daily," as Paul put it. If no one told you that this is what faith walk in ministry would be about, I sympathize with you. Some people think that God's sole purpose is to give us happy, healthy, wealthy, problem-free lives—even in ministry. It comes as a shock to remember the real meaning of discipleship. If you are reeling from that shock, then perhaps you need a reminder of reality. Once your expectations of the ministry life have been brought into line with reality, then God's surprises will no longer be shocks, but become exciting experiences. It's too easy to absorb the world's values and priorities; quite frankly, we are too often self-centered and self-seeking. These things have to be stripped off before our lives in Christ make any sense or offer any real fulfillment.

> Our expectations of the "ministry life" must be in line with reality.

*The Pentecost*—receiving the power to do what I know deep down in my heart I need to do.

In Psalm 23 David recognizes he is a sheep and the Lord is his Shepherd. He affirms that he is led, he is fed, and he is guided along "right paths" for the Shepherd's sake—not his. Goodness and mercy follow him all the days of his life, and when he is devastated by dashed expectations he looks back and sees his Savior smiling at him saying, "This is the way—walk in it!" His shepherd anoints his head with oil—a picture of both healing balm for lumps and bruises engendered through rough terrain and empowerment for the task of being an obedient sheep. His responsibility—as ours—is to follow closely on his heels. If we can do this we shall find that disappointments are often his appointments! The goal, therefore, should be to live in the power of our own personal Pentecost. We need to pray, "God, give me the power to live well in this difficult situation."

## God's Surprises

So here you are, and you can't believe what your life has become. Maybe you did go through a very thorough decision-making process, and maybe you did think you knew what you were getting into, but when you got on the other side of your "yes" you found yourself saying, "Oh, I never expected this."

> God gives us the power to live well in a difficult situation.

But how do you live with it, when you know you are where you should be, but you hate being there? You did not perhaps expect this particular situation—or even the quality of your life in general.

Ministry is one big surprise. So don't be surprised to be surprised! I love the way that God hides the future from us. I wonder if that's one of the things humankind lost in the Garden when we sinned—the ability to see the future. Maybe he knew that we couldn't stand it if we saw what was ahead. Imagine knowing the way you'd die, for instance. You'd spend every day facing that before it happened. And so God in his mercy has veiled the future from us. Whether or not Adam and Eve ever knew it before the Fall we don't know, but we ought to thank the Lord we don't know what's around the corner of tomorrow. Perhaps if we knew the future we'd never step into it. Stuart and I have made our choices carefully, and we feel we have made the right choices, but I don't think we would have been strong enough to say "yes" if we would have known some of the things that were ahead of us.

> We ought to thank the Lord we don't know what's around the corner of tomorrow.

As we walk a step at a time in obedience to God's call, we'll find that the power is there for that one step. If it's God calling, then he is responsible to give us the resources he knows we need to get through. Hold him to that. Although life seldom works out as we expect, it does work out, and it's a bending and enriching thing to experience and to witness together.

> *A good marriage is not one where perfection reigns; it is a relationship where a healthy perspective overlooks a multitude of "unresolvables."*—James Dobson

## When Conflicts Run Deep

But what if you did marry a CPA and would have turned him down if you knew he would go into the ministry in five years? And what if you do feel trapped by this "driven" man you feel you don't know anymore? What then?

In the next chapter, we will address some problems that occur between husbands and wives that are related directly to the wife's role in the ministry. But for now, there is a basic question to be answered: Was this move you made to enter full-time service a huge, painful mistake?

Mistakes *are* made when it comes to making these sort of decisions. Sometimes we are too impatient and choose before it's time. Ecclesiastes says that there is a time for everything. God's clocks keep perfect time, but human beings have been known to impatiently move the hands of God's clock ahead!

## The decision-making process

A lot of books have been written on knowing the "will of God." But as you read, keep in mind that every person's, every couple's journey is different, so we walk on very thin ice when we begin to dictate to others in too much detail how to know what God wants of them. However, I will set out two general principles that I have found to be true.

1. <u>**You must be in regular communication with God and with one another.**</u> God is not some genie that you can ignore most of the time and then "rub the Bible" and summon for the really big events in life. You cannot know God's will apart from being in touch with him. This necessitates maintaining a vital devotional life on a day-to-day basis. You must learn to hear his voice in your "daily doings."

> Walk together, one step at a time, in obedience to God's call.

And you and your spouse must have good communication, too. Talk about your personal Gethsemanes, Calvaries, and Pentecosts. You must work at being honest with one another. You must trust one another's judgment. If there is a difference of opinion you'll need to talk and pray, pray and talk until both can compromise a little and come to a consensus on the issue. All the judgments and decision-making can't be loaded onto one partner or another, because you are a *unit*.

Wives, don't avoid your responsibility by saying, "God will lead my husband, and my husband will lead me." That's not partnership. You both must bear these responsibilities.

**2. Don't underestimate the value of good counselors.** There may be times when what you are convinced God has said will not be popular with anyone. But most of the time he uses counselors to help you in your decisions. These will be people—not necessarily professionals, but godly people— wise in God's Word, people you trust, people who can help you assess the information. Maybe the adviser you need is an expert in finance or legal matters or administration. Or maybe the right counselors are people you are accountable to at church—your pastors or elders. Don't propose to learn God's will in a vacuum. We were placed in the body of believers for a reason. No decision as major as a new thrust in ministry or a career change or a geographic move should be made without sifting through the issues with those in God's family qualified to examine them with you.

> You were placed in the body of believers for a reason. Don't propose to learn God's will in a vacuum.

When Stuart and I were sensing a move from our careers into ministry, we went back to the same godly group of people who had advised us against such a move a few years previously. This time, after prayer, they unanimously told us (individually) that they thought it was "just the right time" to take this momentous step. The book of Proverbs says, "many advisers make victory sure" (Proverbs 11:14).

### An inadequate way to follow God

What I sometimes find among ministry wives is a passivity that often leads to bitterness and dashed expectations. What I mean is that too often it was the husband who decided that God was leading in a certain way, and the wife, per her "duty," followed—not, however, without stifling resentment that was bound to surface later. "Why didn't I tell him what I really felt about the situation?" lamented a young woman after an ill-advised move from one ministry into another.

It would be easy to get into "authority" issues here, but I don't think that's really necessary. The fact is, if you are working in a partnership, being heirs together, the issue is not whether God tells the husband or God tells the wife—or both at the same time. The issue is that everything needs to be worked over in the context of the partnership and before the Lord.

Maybe one of you is hearing God a bit more clearly than the other, so maybe that person first gets the inkling of what God is about to propose. A couple of times I have been the first partner to sense a "move" coming. When Stuart was a banker, enjoying an extremely successful career, we were living in Manchester, England. We were both thoroughly involved in "lay" ministries. I began to feel like a piece of sticky cake stuck to a plate; someone was getting an implement under my life and loosening me around the edges! At that point Stuart did not sense the same restless urge to begin the "detaching"

> You and your spouse are heirs together. You can't operate solely as individuals anymore.

process. That time it was at my instigation that we began to investigate a career change.

Another time it was Stuart coming home from an overseas tour of ministry who confided that he was beginning to "lose the challenge" of the work he was doing and wondered if a spell in the pastorate was being indicated. Now, we call this the "sticky cake principle"!

Once one partner senses the leading of the Lord, then it becomes a matter of the other person hearing and understanding, too, which is a work of the Spirit, not a matter of brow-beating the other partner to comply.

This is a difficult area to explain. You can't just map out a path for people, but what I hope to get across is that God deals with us as heirs together, which means that we can't operate solely as individuals anymore. One partner can't simply decide that "this is God's vision for me and, well, if you want to come along, fine." And I'm afraid this very thing has happened in some form or other in many ministry partnership situations. Other times the man does not even talk his decision over with his wife, feeling it is his job to "get the guidance," and therefore her opinion is superfluous. Women and men coming out of a strict, role-oriented background are especially susceptible to this error. They have been taught that the man must have the first and last word, seeing that he is the God-appointed leader of the household. Therefore, the wife's job is to be a good listener, be submissive and respond, and go along, no matter what. If headship means anything—and I believe it does—then it certainly means that it's the man's responsibility to make sure his wife is equal—and that her input and opinions have equal validity to his.

Good ministry partners operate like heirs in Christ, learning God's plan—together. After all, no one is infallible. It's quite possible that a husband or a wife has understood God incorrectly, has not interpreted the signs quite right. It takes another person to call that into question and thereby come to a balance. It's sort of like the Executive, Legislative, and Judicial branches in government that hold one another in check. Even the leader of an organization needs to have someone with the power to call his decisions into question.

Visions have a quality of malleability. They bend and form as time goes by.

Sometimes the husband or wife has an initial vision that is later altered a bit, tempered and perfected as they go. Since God never shows us the future, and we can never fully understand what's ahead, visions have that quality of malleability—they bend and form as time goes by and as new directions come into focus.

Some of the deep conflicts wives have in regard to expectations and changes in their roles really have to do with their lack of participation in the decision-making process of their marriages. And if you and your husband are in ministry together, you must get this decision-making ironed out. That doesn't mean you will always agree, as partners, but it does mean that you will work hard towards an agreement, that you will work it out together in this mystery called ministry. As Ruth Graham said on one occasion, "If Billy and I agreed on everything, one of us would be unneccessary!"

## What If We're Not Where God Wants Us?

Suppose you discover that you really did make a mistake. You didn't assess the situation, you decided too soon, or one of you railroaded through what you wanted, and now here you are. What do you do now?

First of all, God is quite used to handling our mistakes. He has been dealing with blind, deaf, dumb, impatient, and rebellious people for a long time—some of them leaders, some whose stories of failure are spread out for us in the Scriptures. So if you have made a mistake, it may cost you something, but God *will* provide a way of redemption. He is an old hand at salvaging! He can even "restore the years the locusts have eaten" (Joel 2:25, KJV).

> It may cost you something, but God will provide a way of redemption.

You may have to stay in the situation for a while if a certain commitment has been made. Or you may need to get out now if the Holy Spirit is really sounding the alarm for you to move. Each situation is different. But the important thing is to follow those two general principles: *communicate with God and with each other, and seek help from godly counselors.*

With God, everything has potential. Even in your mistakes there is potential to learn, to grow, and to move on. Don't be defeated, and especially don't blame one another. When a man has come to realize that God didn't mean for him to be in a certain situation after all, that he was jumping the gun or reading in his own desires, the last thing he needs is a vindictive wife who makes him more miserable than ever. Love each other, and get through the rough periods to the next part of the journey. Whatever you do, give yourself a little time to heal and regroup. We don't want to lose you from the ministry!

### Working through surprises

When your expectations have been dashed, that can take the wind right out of your sails for a while. It's not always possible to bounce right back singing, "Praise the Lord!" If you are still trying to catch your breath and adjust to this place where God has put you, you might try the following.

> It's not always possible to bounce right back, singing "Praise the Lord!" if your expectations have been dashed. And that's okay.

1. **Look back at how God has dealt with you in the past.** This often helps you gain a healthier perspective. Think of all the prayers he has answered up to now. This will remind you of God's faithfulness and nip fear in the bud. Satan wants you to be afraid of God's will, so celebrate the way you have come through the past and don't give in to panic. Spend a little time over a meal together, counting your blessings.

2. **Sift out what the real requirements are for your new "position."** If you are replacing a Super Christian and have tremendous expectations heaped upon you, spend some time looking at your own personality, your own gifts, and determine what God wants of you in your particular situation. Be

willing to disappoint others' expectations. Learn who you are and what you are to do and be. If you take on all of their "requirements," the load will probably be too great, as well as ill-fitted for you. Other people (such as those in your pastor-husband's new congregation) also have to take God's surprises in stride, and one of those surprises may be you! Don't underestimate their ability to adjust to you and eventually to love you.

**3. Say whatever you are able to say to God.** God takes us where we are. If all you can say is, *Lord, don't let my pain and anger ruin what you are doing in my husband,* then say that. You may have to pray for God to make you willing to stay with the situation. You may have to ask for help in seeing things in a more positive light. Give God what you can. He will take that and make good with it.

**4. Ask yourself, "What would I rather be doing?"** You may not have a real answer for that. Now is a good time to ask the Holy Spirit to examine you inside and out and help you to sift out some things that are holding you back. Take a look at your values, and evaluate your life goals. With your husband, work through what you both see as a realistic system of goals and priorities. Pray together daily over the areas that are particular problems to you.

> Pray for God to make you willing to work through a realistic system of goals and priorities.

**5. Get at the deeper issues.** Your real problem may be with your own low self-esteem. Or the culprit may be an inadequate system that you and your husband have used in making decisions. You may not be so angry at your husband's lurch into ministry as you are angry that you feel left out of the process. Or your unwillingness and/or fear to serve in this surprise package may be related to other raw nerves in your background. With a counselor, with your spouse, with a close friend, try to get at the real source of frustration. Sometimes it is not as related to the present situation as it appears.

---

*Attempt something so big that unless God intervenes, it is sure to fail.*—Unknown

---

## Who Will Roll the Stone Away?

On the very first Easter morning, some women hurried to the tomb, carrying the spices with which to anoint the body of their Lord. They asked each other, "Who will roll the stone away from the entrance of the tomb?"

When we are in a new, frightening, surprising situation, we face the same problem. We would minister to a loved one perhaps, but a boulder lies in the way. Between us and that dear one a great barrier has appeared, one so big that our puny desires appear ludicrous beside it. Our love seems weak and ineffectual in the face of such an obstacle.

We would dive into this ministry, this package we never expected, but a boulder lies in the way, and we can't possibly imagine how to move it and function in this place.

"Love can't find a way for me; I know, I've tried," you say. Perhaps you face a hostile teenager fed up with being a "minister's kid" and being moved around the country every three years or less. With your hands full of good things—sweet and special presents carefully prepared— you have hurried toward her, only to be confronted with that huge stone of anger, resentment, or misunderstanding.

> Love doesn't give up, and love doesn't run away.

Perhaps you face a cold and unresponsive new church or mission assignment, and, with your hands full of good things—your talents and your dreams—you have reached out to these people, only to be confronted with that huge stone of bland indifference or suspicion. At such a time, you must remember that you don't have all the facts—all the pieces of the puzzle. Perhaps they have lost a former pastor they loved and find it hard to transfer loyalty. Maybe there has been an ugly split in the church or organization. They may be hurting, too.

Jesus' friends must have experienced some of these same feelings. As the women hurried toward that insurmountable "mountain" of trouble that lay ahead of them, they couldn't think of anyone in the whole world except Jesus Christ himself who had the power to roll that stone away; and that was their biggest dilemma—Jesus Christ was dead! They had every right to believe he was lying there, sealed into ineffectiveness by the very stone they confronted.

Perhaps you face a seemingly immovable object in fear, an object that you have no power to move. Maybe you believe that the God you had trusted is unable to help you this time. You may be stymied with a sense of inadequacy. You may even be tempted to give up and run away! But love doesn't give up, and love doesn't run away. Love always walks on, even when it believes the object of its love is dead.

The thing to do in the face of insurmountable problems is to walk right on up to them with every intention of walking right on through them, even if they show no signs of yielding as you approach. If you can't walk through, walk around—find a way past to the Lord, who may or may not move the stone or intervene on your behalf. Somehow we need to live life with the attitude, "I love the Lord; my hands are full of gifts for him; and one way or the other, I will find him on the other side of the problem." It's certain that you'll never arrive at the other side of your problem by running away from it! So face it; face it together with your partner and with any other believers you

> Walk right on up to your problems with every intention of walking right through them.

can find with the same heartbeat—the same vision. And don't waste energy apportioning blame. If you do that, you'll exhaust yourself before you ever get there!

I have spent so many years anticipating the blockages ahead and practicing rolling them away in my imagination. I have tried to peer apprehensively into the future, convinced there are mountains to move just out of sight. "Don't borrow what hasn't happened," advised a dear friend of mine as she saw me struggling to move an obstacle that I believed would face me six months into the future. "Why don't you wait until you get there, will you?" continued my good friend. "Somebody who knows about these things has discovered that eighty percent of the things we worry about never happen anyway!" She was right, of course. We may as well be using that energy to worry about the stones that have been rolled in front of us instead of the ones that might or probably never will.

The women hurried on that early morning toward that huge rock that separated them from the body of their beloved Christ. They were frightened, yes, but they kept going. They went anyway. Don't wait until you are unafraid before you walk up to the sepulcher. If you can't walk up to it unafraid, walk up to it afraid. And maybe, just maybe, when you get there, you will find that the stone has been rolled away.

> Christ cannot be contained within the tombs of our troubles, inside the sepulchers of our sorrows, or behind the doors of our doubts. No stone can shut him up or take him away from his disciples.

Christ cannot be contained within the tombs of our troubles, inside the sepulchers of our sorrows, or behind the doors of our doubts. No stone can shut him up or take him away from his disciples. The stone still stood there in that quiet garden, a reminder of the reality of the problems we all must live with; but Christ had moved it to one side so very easily, demonstrating his resurrection power on our behalf.

You must face your personal Gethsemane and die at your Calvary. But all is not lost. Look toward your Pentecost, the power that will come. Rejoice, for "THE STONE HAS BEEN ROLLED AWAY!"

---

*Roll the stone away, Lord Jesus,*
*Roll the stone away!*
*I hurry to the trouble*
*Before the break of day.*
*I wake in the night watches,*
*I pray with grief and tears;*
*I cry into my pillow*
*And rehearse my doubts and fears.*
*But if I'll stop and listen*
*And if I'll do my part*
*An angel will address me*
*And speak peace unto my heart.*
*He'll say "Why are you unhappy?*
*The Lord is risen indeed;*
*The stone has been removed*
*and Jesus Christ will meet your need!"*
—Jill Briscoe

## ■ For Further Information . . .

*Stick a Geranium in Your Hat and Be Happy!* by Barbara Johnson. Word, Inc., 1990.
Life isn't always what you want . . . but it's what you've got! If you need a fresh breath of joy in your life, this book is just the prescription for you. Barbara Johnson can help you look for "life's little sparkles," even in the midst of the most crippling sorrows. Despite her difficulties, Barbara has learned that though pain is inevitable, we can choose to pick the flowers instead of the weeds.

# 6

# When Your Gifts Don't Fit Your Role

SUCCESSFUL MARRIAGE IS ALWAYS A TRIANGLE;
A MAN, A WOMAN, AND GOD.
—*CECIL MYERS*

When Stuart and I first came to Elmbrook (our present church), I fell into a ministry quite innocently. One day a woman came to my door and said, "Your husband announced from the pulpit, 'If anyone would like to come see us, just drop by.' Well, here I am. I dropped by."

And I said, "Oh, do come in." So she came in and told me that she was a new believer, and she had some friends. She wondered if I would come and talk to them about the Lord if she got them all together. I told her I would be delighted.

So that's how an all-women's ministry began—with just six women, the friends of this lady. Well, after a while the group grew to about thirty in number, and I said to them one day, "Where do you sit in church, because I never see you there on Sunday? Don't you come?" And one of them said very shyly, "Well, we didn't like to tell you, but most of us don't go to your church. We go to this other church, and the pastor doesn't believe the Bible quite like you do. I don't even know if he thinks there is a devil. We knew that if we told you where we go and what we believe you might stop teaching us, so we didn't tell you."

There I sat, this new pastor's wife fresh from England, thinking that these were the women who went to our church and having now discovered that they didn't. But they had all found the Lord, so what was I to do with them?

I went home and said to Stuart, "You've no idea what I've done." And I told him all about it.

Stuart said, "They're all finding the Lord. That's great. Let's just let the river cut its own channel. We'll see what happens."

"But what will our church ladies think?" I questioned.

And he replied, "I can tell you already that they don't think much of it but never mind. Just go ahead with it; I'll look after the rest."

So, under my husband's encouragement, I got on with it, using the gifts God had given me—gifts that did not fit the role that was expected of me in our church. The ministry took off—exploded, ending up after a couple of years with about seven hundred women.

> Sometimes a ministry just happens, and you are overjoyed at seeing people change and grow in the Lord.

Since the majority didn't belong to our fellowship at first and I wasn't connected with any of theirs, I had to seek out neutral places to meet, so we used a bank and then a theater, which we filled. I was overjoyed with seeing women change and grow in the Lord.

Then the honeymoon ended. Some of the women in my church, several of them prominent members, began saying, "What is she doing? She's ours. She should be teaching the women's Sunday school class." Well, they had a wonderful lady teaching the women's Sunday school class, and I didn't want to take her job. Besides, I don't like teaching women's Sunday school classes very much. I love evangelizing women. So that's what I was doing.

Then came the time when Stuart and I were invited for a meal with the elders and their wives. I was naive and thought, *Oh how fun! An evening of food and fellowship with the elders and their wives.* And the meal was very nice. Only at the end of it the chairman of the board said to my husband, "We really brought you here tonight to talk about what Jill is doing."

In a nutshell, they wanted me to stop my women's meetings, at least meetings with that particular group. There were a number of other things they thought I should be doing.

My husband listened quietly through all this. As for me, I shrank smaller and smaller in my chair, wanting to die so that Stuart could have an American wife who could do all the right things!

But Stuart suddenly said, "You know, if you insist in telling my wife what to do, then I will insist in telling your wives what to do. Is that understood?" Then I *really* wanted to die. I thought that with this remark I had probably lost all the friends I might have had around the table.

Then Stuart continued: "Look, you hired me, not my wife. She started this in all innocence. She responded to a lady coming to the door, and we had no idea what it was going to lead to. Isn't it incredible what's happening? Couldn't you women get behind her and help her? If you let her be who she is and use the gifts God gave her, she will be a huge blessing to the fellowship."

> "Let her be who she is and she will be a blessing."

That was a small turning point. The pressure was off me, and I was free to do what it seemed God had called me to. And some of those women that night became my coworkers. But, you see, my husband insisted that I exercise my gift for the good of the body, even though it didn't fit the expected role. Some people never did understand, and I did lose some friends. You have to accept such losses; they happen in ministry. Some people will never understand the role that God has gifted you to fill in a particular situation because they don't

> You simply have to do your best and leave the rest to God.

*want* to understand! In a way, your gifts should determine your role. You simply have to do your best and leave the rest to him. Your best can't always be good enough for some people, but you have to be what you were meant to be.

## A Picture from Jesus

Think about a little boat, one with a water line around it. A water line is drawn on the outside by the maker of the craft to indicate how deep in the water the boat should be sitting. If the water is over the water line, then there is too much weight in the boat, and it's going to sink. On the other hand, if it's sitting high above the water line, it will be "unfulfilled." Think of yourself as a little boat.

Most boats have some kind of flag on the tops of their masts. Right now maybe all that is showing of your boat is a little white flag. You've sunk way below the water line. Even while you are reading this book you may be so overloaded that you are sinking. Or maybe this isn't the case at all. You are perhaps floating high above the water line. You're unfulfilled; you're carrying hardly anything that you've been created to carry.

> The whole idea of partnership in marriage is to get us balanced— "loaded" right.

The whole idea of this partnership in marriage is to get us balanced, "loaded" right, according to the way we are made. Jesus put it this way: "Come unto Me all you who are overladen and I will give you "rest" (or balance). Yoked to me, close to me, I'll show you the burdens you're meant to bear" (Matthew 11:28, my paraphrase). In case you're wondering, I really am not putting anything into the

Scriptures here, because Jesus did use a term that is used in Acts to describe the unloading of cargo off a boat. Most of Jesus' disciples were fishermen, and when he said, "Come to me, all you who are weary or *burdened*," I imagine they got the message.

That's a wonderful picture to me because I think of all of us as different kinds of boats, and therefore it follows that all of us need to carry different kinds of cargo. Some of us are battleships, and some of us are cargo vessels, and some of us perhaps are like little skiffs that cannot carry very much at all but delight people with our personalities and beauty. I often say to Stuart, "I think you're the Titanic." And he says, "Thanks. That sank, you know." He doesn't appreciate that at all! But the point is, we are made *differently*. Think about it: I stand in church on Sundays and watch all the boats come in to worship. I wouldn't be very wise to think, as I watch a big battleship come through the door, that the little skiff that follows the big battleship into church should carry the same responsibilities. When I see the beautiful little skiff come through the doors, how stupid I would be if I suggested she take some of the cannons from the battleship and turn herself into a "man o' war"!

> Some of us are battle-ships, and some of us are cargo vessels, and some of us are little skiffs.

Do you see what I'm getting at? It's a matter of each person's uniqueness before God. God is the craftsman, and he put the water line around us. He knows us far better than we know ourselves or each other. He is not nearly as concerned with roles as we are, but he is concerned with the gifts he gave to us. He is disappointed when we let those gifts go to waste.

What kind of boat do you think you are? Does it give you real joy to be with people all the time, listening to their stories, taking on big emotional cargo? If so, then that's the kind of

vessel you were made to be, able to carry a lot of those kinds
of burdens.

But what if you aren't that kind of boat at all? "My emotional resources are very limited in that area," you may say. "Of
course I am committed to serving people,
ministering to them, but I work best in
solitude." My guess is that if this is your
personality, then some of the gifts God has
given you are best manifested in a more
private space. Maybe you're a fantastic or-
ganizer—a detail person—who can suc-
cessfully juggle all the data and logistics
that go into a church-wide Sunday school or a community
welfare program, and you work best in the quiet of your
home. Maybe you're good with computers, with things on
paper. Perhaps you're an artistic type of person, and if you
were free and encouraged to develop those gifts, the church
would be brimming with your creativity in the form of flower
arrangements, drama, congregational readings, or colorful
church banners.

> God is not
> nearly as
> concerned
> with roles as
> we are.

Ask yourself two very, very important questions. One,
"What gifts and talents do I have?" and two, "Do they fit my
role?" If you don't know what your gifts are (and that
knowledge doesn't come naturally just because you are a ministry wife), or if your gifts don't fit your present role—it's time
to talk it out with God and with your spouse!

---

Husbands, in the same way be considerate as you
live with your wives, and treat them with respect as
the weaker partner and as heirs with you of the
gracious gift of life, so that nothing will hinder your
prayers. *1 Peter 3:7*

## Your Husband's Responsibility

Part of your husband's responsibility is to see to it that you are carrying the proper kind of load. After all, humanly speaking, who knows you better (outside of maybe your parents)? He should understand how you operate best, and that should give him intimate insight on how he can help you reach your potential without overloading. He can make sure you don't take on too much of a load. He's the one who lives with you and sees when you've begun to sink. People in your church are not likely to see this; they will only notice it after you've gone under for the second or third time. So it's up to the husband, primarily, to keep a loving, considerate, and watchful eye on his wife, for he is the one who knows her in the deepest sense.

In 1 Peter 3, Peter is talking about two things that a husband should do for his wife: respect her weaknesses and honor her strengths.

### *Respecting weaknesses*

What is this weakness the husband is to respect? Have you ever figured out what Peter meant by that? What does it mean that we're the "weaker" vessels, as the King James Version puts it ("partners" in NIV)? This is a good topic of conversation for the supper table for you and your husband to tackle together!

> What does it mean that we are the "weaker vessel"?

Does it mean we are weaker physically? Statistics show that women live a lot longer then men, so I don't think it can mean that. Of course in some types of strength—how much we can bench press, for example—women are obviously weaker. But we are strong enough to carry and bear children. And if you look at the people who survive disasters and long-term mistreatment, there is evidence that women have more stamina over the long haul.

Could we be weaker intellectually? Do you think so? I don't. Are women weaker intellectually than men? No. There's been absolutely no evidence ever presented to hold up a statement like that. Because of our position in society through the centuries, we've not been in the intellectual limelight as much as men or had the same intellectual stimulation or training available as our counterparts. That is a cultural limitation, nothing inherent as to who we are or what we can achieve.

Weaker emotionally, then? I've met some pretty brave women, haven't you? And in a crisis, I'm sure you know that women can be very, very strong indeed. I look into the faces of some women with whom I deal day in and day out and say, "How did you even find the emotional strength to get dressed and come here today?" because of the psychological (and sometimes physical) battering they're taking at home. We have hundreds of single parents in our church fellowship, and many of them are among the most courageous people I know. So I don't think we are weaker emotionally. The NIV *Study Bible* opts for the physical strength option. It says that the fact that Peter refers to the weaker partner is "not a reference to moral stamina, strength of character or mental capacity but most likely to sheer physical strength" (p. 1892).

I would like to add a new thought to the debate. Part of our physical stamina is tied up with our sexuality. I do believe that when Peter calls us the weaker vessel he means weaker *sexually*. I believe it because this particular word "vessel" (KJV) in 1 Peter 3 is only used in one other place and that's where Paul talks about sexuality to the Thessalonians and tells them to keep their vessels (bodies) sexually pure (1 Thessalonians 4:4). In this area we are weaker. We are definitely vulnerable in ways men are not because of our sexual

> Women are sexually vulnerable.

make-up. We carry and bear children, we experience monthly hormonal influences we can do little about. This feminine sexuality is a wonderful, unfathomable gift God has given us as women, and it carries special blessings and responsibilities. But it can also limit us in other ways. Sometimes we just do not have the wherewithal to control our emotions, or mood swings, especially at certain points in our menstrual cycle. We can't pretend that these aspects of our lives don't affect us.

The husband needs to nurture, love, and be considerate of his wife in this regard. He needs to understand her *sexuality*, for that is often the point of her greatest stress and weakness.

Not long ago I made similar remarks at a pastors and wives conference. Afterwards the men lined up to tell me funny jokes about PMS! I wondered if they had heard me or had any clue how their wives felt about those jokes. I'm all for being able to laugh at ourselves, but I don't think that those who suffer the real trauma of PMS think it is a laughing matter!

Put on top of all this the normal pressures that go with the territory of being a ministry wife. There are times when we are especially vulnerable, and a husband can learn to be sensitive to that. Maybe he should check the calendar before he brings ten people home to supper—wait until after those few days have passed. I mean it; why should this be embarrassing to discuss with a husband? Why shouldn't he take these things into account? After all, he wouldn't bring in the hordes if you were down with the flu, would he? And

> Maybe your husband should check the calendar before he brings ten people home for supper!

for some women the biological cycle can be as rough as or rougher than that. Pregnancy and caring for an infant and small children—although we certainly shouldn't compare those to illness!—also take their toll on a woman physically and emotionally. This is all part of a man really "knowing" his wife. If only he understands what a woman goes through and what happens when her hormones are in an uproar, then he can "be" her strength at the low points.

In other words, our husbands should know us that well. They should respect our weaknesses.

We can take the pressure off of each other in the ministry by anticipating such things and giving each other space when needed. Happy is the woman who has such a partner. Then there is the question of honoring our strengths.

---

*A well-known preacher delivered a sermon before a congregation in which his wife was a worshiper. When the service was over, he went over to her and asked, "How did I do?" She replied, "You did fine, only you missed several opportunities to sit down."*—Asbury Lenox

---

### Honoring strengths

Awhile ago, a ministry wife tearfully confided in me: "I want to help. He is in over his head. He's doing everything." The "he" she was referring to was her husband, and he was the pastor of a small church. As the wife told me, "I know I could help with lots of things if only he'd let me, but he won't allow me to do anything, not even be constructively critical!"

"He's doing everything; I know I could help with lots of things if only he'd let me!"

Why? Many husbands won't like one possible answer that I'm going to give. Often it's because the man is threatened. Maybe he knows his wife has certain spiritual gifts and that she could do some of the things he is doing better than he could.

Let me give you a real-life example. One woman I talked to was an absolute whiz with money; her husband was *not*. Any financial details were a headache to him—dealing with them was a chore. It took him hours. Sadly, she shared with me the following words: "If only he would just give me that whole side of things, I could take the burden off him, but he won't let it go." Why? In that particular instance it was because he was threatened by his wife's abilities.

A man of quality is never threatened by a woman of equality. Men who release their wives to be all Christ meant them to be must be willing to let their spouses go in their particular directions of giftedness. And they will need the humility to say, "Look, I'm really not very good at this. Why don't you give it a try? Do you think you could help me with it?" (By the way, wives, this works both ways!)

> A man of quality is never threatened by a woman of equality.

Part of a husband's job is to challenge his wife to develop those talents, those gifts that will be useful in the partnership and useful to God's work in their specific local fellowship or mission. The challenging goes along with nurturing and protecting.

I thank the Lord for my husband who has always insisted that I develop gifts I didn't even know I had. That has been part of his (he feels) God-given duty. He wrote an article about a woman's gifts for *Moody Monthly** years ago that is still bringing us letters of response (and reaction). On the cover of the magazine was a burial urn. Stuart's basic message was: The Bible says we must not bury our gifts. Most men know that, but what does the Bible say if we bury somebody else's gifts, like the women in our congregations or our lives?

My husband doesn't want to bury women's ministry gifts and believes he will be answerable to God for that. Stuart wrote about two women in his life that he felt were very gifted—his wife and his daughter. He has considered himself responsible for nurturing our gifts and setting us free.

*This article is included on pp. 93-98.

*Nurturing, encouraging, setting free.* You could say that the husband is sort of a coach, and if he sees a play and knows somebody is gifted to execute it, he'll send that person into the game and expect the rest of the team to be supportive. In the same way a man discerns the gifts of the women in the family, figuring out how their strengths can win the day. This way he is honoring her.

> Use whatever gift you have received to serve others.

Take a look at 1 Peter 4:10. "Each one should use whatever gift he has received to serve others, faithfully administering God's grace in its various forms." Notice that it doesn't say "each husband" or "each man." Each *one.* A glance at the context tells you that Peter is writing to men and women—each *believer.* Each should use his or her gift. Each should use whatever that gift is to serve others.

## A Tension between Gifts and Roles

What happens when your gift doesn't fit the role you've been placed in or the role it *appears* you've been placed in? Note that 1 Peter 4:10 doesn't say that "each one should use the gift that fits the role to serve others." The "role" can be all sorts of different things. The "role" in one church is not the same as the "role" in another church. The expectations of any particular congregation are wrapped up in the church's past culture and roots and the past ministry wives who have served that particular fellowship. If a woman finds herself talented and gifted in a way that does not fit that particular role for that particular congregation there could be a bit of a problem.

I heard a true story in Brazil. It was told to me through an interpreter by a pastor's wife. She and her husband had followed a church planting couple who had been a dynamic duo. Church planters go in, start a church, then move on to start another, and so on. This pastor and wife happened to follow this Bionic Christian Couple. Some of you know what I'm talking about, don't you? They had been the type of couple who are just impossible to follow because they're so unusually gifted and successful. You have the feeling that the people sort of dread seeing *you* come along because you couldn't be half as good as Mr. and Mrs. Bionic. Perhaps you are in this situation right now.

This young woman was totally different than the pastor's wife she followed, and she felt desperately inadequate and very worried. However, she was willing to try to step into and fill those huge shoes left to her. They had only been there a week when she got up one morning, looked out the window, and saw a long line of men outside her door. It seemed the whole village was there! She went to her husband and said, "The men of the village are waiting in a line at the door. What do you think they want?"

> "I was trying to be this wonderful ministry wife and fill these huge shoes."

"I don't know," her husband replied. "Ask them."

So she opened the door hesitantly and asked, "What do you want?"

The man at the head of the line was standing there with a stool and a pair of scissors. One of them said, "The previous pastor's wife cut all the men's hair in the village. That's why we're here."

The pastor's wife nearly fainted on the spot. She had never cut anybody's hair in her life. She wasn't at all practical with her hands. She ran back to her husband and blurted out the information, and he said, "Well, just try."

So the first one sat down and she did quite well. She was getting all excited. Maybe she *could* cut hair—perhaps it was a gift she didn't know she had. But as she relaxed a bit she grew careless and in the process, she chopped off the top of a fidgety man's ear! He had to be flown out by helicopter to be attended to.

This poor little lady told me all this, nearly in tears. She said, "You know, here I was, trying to be this wonderful pastor's wife, trying to do the same things the last one had done, trying to fulfill the expectations. And it wasn't working."

You see, not only does the congregation have expectations of you coming from their own cultural church backgrounds, but they have expectations of you drawn from their experiences with the previous minister's wife.

As for me and Elmbrook, I followed a nearly perfect role model of a pastor's wife. Naturally it was difficult for the church to accept me as I was. Eventually, with my husband's help, I was able to face them and say, "If you will let me be who God has gifted me to be, then I will really be able to contribute, and that includes letting me exercise gifts that don't fit the role here. But if you don't allow me to do that and you insist on me doing things that I am not gifted to do, I will be no good to anybody and we will all end up being frustrated."

> Allow each other to be strong where you are strong.

We had that confrontation. It wasn't easy. It was not without tears on both sides, but in the end we decided to allow one another to use the gifts we had been given and to be strong where we were strong. As a result, we have one of the most exciting women's ministries, I believe, in the whole of North America. God has enabled me to stimulate others to think creatively and to do what hadn't been done before.

> We've got to recognize the art of the possible in ministry.

Remember: we are all meant to carry a burden—a "cargo." Something Jesus asks us to carry for him. When Jesus said, "My burden is easy," he didn't mean what we think of today as easy. The word he used would be better translated "possible." The art of the "possible" in ministry is what we've got to get to. How to balance that, how to find the possible, is something I'll talk about in the next chapter.

So nourish each other's weaknesses, but honor each other's strengths. Explore the talents and gifts that make you the person God created you to be. And then exercise them, with each other's help and encouragement.

---

*Cynthia once told me, "You know, Honey, it's not right to tell people we're partners. You don't let me enter into your ministry. You don't share." That cut me like a knife. But I couldn't challenge her. She had the goods on me. I've always admired that about Cynthia—she will always tell me the truth, even when it hurts. And truth is what sets you free.*—Charles Swindoll

---

## Partners Who Complement One Another

A psychologist once said to Stuart and me, after a conference we had done together, "I love it when you and Stuart speak one after the other. I've never seen such an example of right brain/left brain in my life." (I'm glad he didn't say "half brain/no brain"!) What he was getting at is that he didn't sense any competition between us. He felt that we complemented each other. Our gifts are similar enough that we are able to teach as a team. Not everyone is gifted for team ministry, and if you try it without the gifts it can be a disaster—but generally Stuart goes for the head and I go for the heart. And if he sees something I've missed he can cover it, and vice-versa.

> Not everyone is gifted for team ministry.

In any case it will take time to find the balance; sometimes people with similar gifts have trouble working together. Stuart has learned to let me talk on in my right-brained way, and I have learned to let him go on in his left-brained way. We don't expect each other to change our styles of relating. If either one of us insisted that everything be taught the same way, then we would have real problems. But in marriage, and especially in a ministry partnership, we have learned not merely to accept basic differences of personality, but actually to encourage those differences and to see them as adding color and variety. As two people with very different ways of doing things, we automatically get to twice as many people in a given crowd as just one of us would.

It is so important that you spend time with your husband and the Lord together, sifting through things like personality, style, and your own sense of what God wants you to do and how you think it can be accomplished. And I'm not talking about just reading a book together on personality types or spiritual gifts, although that may be helpful. It's not as simple as that. These things come from time with the Lord, with one another, in deep, searching prayer and honest communication. It will certainly mean risking a little. You may be an introvert, for example, but God may be calling you to do something not-so-introverted. When you walk with God, there are always those sorts of surprises. So you can't just go into a situation with the idea, "Well, that's just not my thing," or saying, "I know I don't have that gift." In general, God will want you to do the things for which he has given you a natural and specialized talent. But we must never forget that we should be totally dependent upon his wisdom and his timing in our lives, and it may well be that we have gifts we are not even aware of. The arena of ministry often gives us a chance to discover them!

> It may well be we have gifts and talents we are not even aware of.

Both Stuart and I have done many different things during our lives, and they weren't always things that made us comfortable. But if a couple can find God's work for both of them, not compete with one another but rather complement the other, then neither will feel threatened. This will take a lot of extra energy, but remember that God never "calls" without equipping.

> *Sometimes we have the mistaken idea*
> *that love is like automatic cruise control—*
> *you push a button, lean back, relax*
> *and enjoy the ride. But if love is going to work,*
> *I must be willing to put something*
> *into the relationship, not just*
> *take from it.*—Ruth Senter

## A Word from My Husband Stuart . . .

The most difficult things for men to say are, "I'm sorry," "I was wrong," and "I'm scared." Confession being good for the soul, let me state here and now that I need to say all those things—at the same time! Let me explain.

I was raised in a church setting where women were not encouraged to minister in any way other than menial. As I had never thought about, much less studied the issue, I had imbibed the conventional wisdom and followed the party line. But then I met Jill who had never heard what I had heard and when she did, wished she hadn't! Her obvious abilities and effectiveness in ministry to difficult teenagers pushed me into a much-needed study of a woman's place in ministry. As a result I had to say to her and many other women, "I'm sorry, I was wrong." Being very masculine, saying "I'm scared" took time, but eventually I admitted that I was not at all sure what was going to happen. That was long ago and I'm so glad. Now

I'm not scared of encouraging women to minister, but I'm still scared I might be a hindrance to them.

### Buried treasure

Pity the man in Scripture (see Matthew 25:14-30) who buried his talent. He knew what he had, and he knew what he could do with it. But he decided to bury it. Perhaps he was too tired, too lazy, too fearful or too conservative. We don't know, but we do know he missed his chance.

His master was upset. The servant had wasted his substance in non-involvement.

This servant rocked no boats, but then he crossed no oceans. Although he challenged no positions, neither did he create anything new. Instead, he confused investment with interment.

| What does the Bible say about burying a woman's gifts? |
| :---: |

And what about the one who buries someone else's talent? Should we pity that person too? Suppose, for instance, that the master gives one of his female servants a talent but then buries it so that she cannot use what he has given.

Some of us think that, in many instances, the church may be doing just that—burying the talents of the Master's female servants.

That they are talented goes without saying. But we'll say it anyway. Joel said it, Peter repeated it, Paul taught it, and common sense insists on it.

We know the Holy Spirit gifts all believers, including women, for the upbuilding of the church and the glory of God.

The Master has great numbers of female servants, or handmaidens, as they used to be called. They usually outnumber the men in worship services, prayer meetings, mission stations, and church kitchens.

They seem to have a great heart for the Lord; they love to study the Word of God and are eager to pray.

But even though they are so numerous and so interested, the full force of their cumulative talents doesn't seem to have been released. So great has been the burial that some of us think the greatest wasted resource in the church is woman-power.

No doubt, someone will say, "You are contradicting yourself. If they are in the services and the meetings, the missions and the kitchens, how can their talents be buried?"

Their presence, however, does not guarantee participation, and participation does not necessarily mean the fullest investment of talent.

So maybe we need to acknowledge the possibility that many of the people in our churches—the women—are not using their talents as they should, not necessarily because they don't want to but because they are not allowed to. If this is true, it is serious, especially for those who might be doing the burying.

> A talent is a terrible thing to waste.

Some talents lie buried because they have never been unearthed. They have not been consciously buried. They have simply never been explored.

My mother, for example, was a talented woman; but her upbringing was such that she never found it out until almost too late. She had definite ideas about "the woman's place" and settled down to fulfilling her perceived role.

But late in life, she had to do things she had never done before—things she thought women should not do. But out of necessity she did them and to her amazement found herself wonderfully gifted.

Her father had maintained definite ideas about the woman's place, ideas she dared not question. Her husband held similar views, and her church rigidly adhered to the mindset that assumed she was unsuited for anything except having babies and serving salmon sandwiches. It would also insist she was a deaf mute.

All along, however, she had a keen mind, an articulate tongue, a creative energy, and a strong determination. But as far as her church was concerned, those abilities lay buried most of her life. She wholeheartedly supported her husband and wonderfully raised her boys, but she had much more to give that she was never allowed to share.

Why should this be the case for so many women? There are many possible answers, but sincere theological conviction undoubtedly tops the list. In the light of some aspects of biblical teaching, many committed believers are convinced that the woman's role in the church is very limited. I don't question their sincerity, but I do wonder how they explain God's apparent gifting of women for tasks they are not allowed to fulfill?

> God has gifted women for many types of tasks.

Another possible answer is the many men who are struggling with what they perceive as "women's lib" in ecclesiastical garb. They don't like to acknowledge that many highly vocal and visible women have made their secular points.

They don't like it that the modern business community, for so long a male preserve, has seen an invasion of highly gifted, ambitious, and attractive women. Having those kinds of challenges in the office and the political arena is bad enough for them without the hassle in church meetings, too.

One man, whom I greatly admire, told me, "Frankly, I'm tired of seeing women take over our church."

Another reason, of course, is tradition. Traditionally, the church's talented woman has had little opportunity to show what she can do.

But how great are the women who are an exception to the rule. Women certainly played a significant role in the ministry springing from John Wesley. How can we overlook the band of Salvation Army girls recruited by William Booth, who unabashedly said, "Most of my best men are women."

And who can gainsay Gladys Aylward, Corrie ten Boom, Isabel Kuhn, Helen Roseveare, and Amy Carmichael, to name but a few?

Tradition is certainly valuable to provide continuity; but when that continuity heads in the wrong direction, it can be disastrous. Fortunately, however, Christians have been more adept at switching their traditional positions than they probably realize.

Who, today, would agree: "Woman is a necessary evil, a national temptation, a desirable calamity, a domestic peril, a deadly fascination and a painted ill." That quote comes from John Chrysostom, the fourth century's golden-mouthed preacher.

And who holds to this? "If a woman becomes weary, or at last dead from childbearing, that matters not; she is there to do it."

Our old friend Martin Luther.

John and Martin, great theologians that they were, undoubtedly "proved" their points from Scripture, but no doubt a heavy layer of tradition overshadowed their theology. Having changed as far as we have from their view, perhaps one day we will look back at our own traditions and find them not as sound as we had fondly imagined.

> Perhaps one day we will look back at our own traditions about women and find them not as sound as we fondly imagined.

Frankly, as a pastor, a husband, and a father, I have a dread of burying someone else's talents, particularly those bestowed on women.

Accordingly, I have tried to scrutinize my views, the place of tradition, the thrust of theology, and the force of my prejudices. Repeatedly, I have come back to this fact: If the Lord has given gifts, I had better be careful about denying freedom for their exercise.

> Encourage the differences in your personalities; they add color and variety.

More than that, I need to ensure that the women in my life have every encouragement from me to be what he called and gifted them to be. A major part of my life must be spent as a man caring for, nurturing, encouraging, and developing gifted women, because they aren't the only ones who will give account for their stewardship.

As a man in a male-oriented church, I may one day be asked about their gifts, too. I would like to be able to say I did considerably more than burying.

A talent is a terrible thing to waste.*

*Adapted from "Buried Treasure," Stuart Briscoe, *Moody Monthly*, February, 1983.

# ■ For Further Information . . .

*Resource Guide for Women's Ministries: Discover Your Place for Ministry,* by Linda R. McGinn. Broadman Press, 1990.

# 7

# Finding A Balance

MY GOAL IS GOD HIMSELF, NOT JOY NOR PEACE,
NOR EVEN BLESSING, BUT HIMSELF, MY GOD.
—OSWALD CHAMBERS

Have you noticed that when you are asked to give a talk on the Christian family the kids usually try to murder each other before you leave to speak? I well remember shouting at our three as I tried to "untangle " their flailing bodies before I went out to speak about "peace and harmony in the home"! Or you are asked to give a testimony about faith, and you want to wear gloves because your nails are bitten down to the quick.

It's a little bit the same when trying to talk about priorities. This is an area of confusion in my life most weeks! But I have learned some basic principles I can apply each time to assess the situation and hopefully get my priorities straight.

The area of priorities is one of the most difficult there is to address because what we're really talking about is balance. Women are constantly wondering what they are to be doing, and how much, and in what proportion. There is a lot of work to be done in God's kingdom, and we can never run out of things to do, but we can and do run out of strength and sanity to do them all at once. Of course, we were

> You will never run out of things to do.

never meant to do everything at the same time; we see what happens to people who try to be Super Nova Christians. Super Novas are huge stars that have so much pressure building up inside them that they finally "implode"—disintegrating internally. Know any people in ministry who fit that description? But at the same time, how do we rearrange our priorities so that we are doing what God would wish us to do? God has specific things in mind for each of us, and we need to know which things and in what order. Because women have so many more opportunities open to them now in terms of ministry, many ministry wives struggle daily and painfully with the issue of balance.

I asked myself once, "Where can I find a model for this balancing act?" And it seemed to me that the safest place to start was with Jesus.

## Jesus' Balanced Life

It says in Luke's gospel that Jesus increased in wisdom and stature, in favor with God, and in favor with man. He was balanced—intellectually, physically, spiritually, and socially. Jesus grew up balanced. What was the key to his balanced life? We know so little about those thirty years in Nazareth. I want to ask the Scriptures, "Tell me more."

> Jesus grew up balanced— what was the key?

But we don't have more. All we know is that he grew intellectually, physically, spiritually, and socially. The only words we have of his from those days were spoken in the temple when he was twelve and at a moment when his parents thought he was not where he should be. He said: "I must be about my Father's business" (Luke 2:49). That's the only thing we know he said; otherwise there are thirty years of silence.

So at least we know that from a very early age the priority for Jesus was his Father's business. So let's apply that. What must *I* be doing? My Father's business. Not my business, not your business, not the church's business, and not the family's business. *His* business. The Father's business might include all of those other things, but unless I have it clearly in my head that the priority of my life is my Father's business, I am not going to do very well with this balancing act.

I have thought long and hard about the question: *What was the Father's business?* I believe the answer to that is the redemption of the world. That "business" works itself out in all sorts of ways and through all sorts of people, but the overarching purpose of God is just that: the redemption of the world.

So, if you are a mother at home with preschool children, what is the key to your being balanced? The answer is that you must be "about your Father's business." And what is that? The redemption of the world. And you should carry out that priority above all else in all your mothering, in all you do for your children. Don't let anybody rob you of that. Let the Sunday school teacher follow up the privilege you have to lead your own child to Christ.

> Your Father's business is the redemption of the world.

To be aware that "today" may be the day you as a Christian mother lead your own child to Jesus Christ will keep you on your spiritual toes in the midst of the "Viet Nam" in the living room, the hectic grocery shopping with tiny children catapulting off in every direction, the clean-up time after supper. All three of our children came to Christ during "daily days." One at lunch, one in the car after a shopping trip, and one while I was baking. Lunch, shopping, and baking were priorities but not the main one. The main priority for me as a Christian mom was to keep myself available to the Holy Spirit to use if he wished to bring the message of redemption to my kids. "I must be about my Father's business" meant, for me, having the incredible privilege of leading two of our three little ones to Christ at the age of four!

When you have young children, you wake up with that priority of your Father's business. You go to bed with it. You get in the bathtub with it, you wash the diapers with it, you take the kids out with it, you go shopping with it. "I must be about my Father's business" has got to be your priority.

| The priority of your life must be your Father's business. |

For thirty years Jesus pleased the people who watched him. Everybody thought well of him; they said, "He's a wise little boy asking these great big spiritual people wonderful questions." He was growing spiritually and intellectually. He was strong enough to be a superb carpenter. He was in favor with God, in favor with people.

## Jesus' Unbalanced Life

All of Jesus' life, according to the people around him, was balanced—until he went into the ministry. And suddenly, according to this world, Jesus became the most unbalanced person around. Mark 3:20 says: "Jesus entered a house, and again a crowd gathered, so that he and his disciples were not even able to eat."

I did some cross-referencing and found other such statements in the Gospels.

Once when I was speaking I used an illustration about being on a ministry trip and always being hungry. This was because a packed schedule had me on a plane when I should have been eating. After my speech, a lady came up to me and said, "I'm worried about you that you miss meals. Do you think that's biblical?" And I said, "Well, I just happen to know that sometimes it is!" Then I showed her Mark 3:20.

Sometimes when the crowd gathers you have no alternative—you miss a meal. People say, "Now, that's not balanced."

Or, "How can it be right if it causes you discomfort?" Somebody told me the other day that you shouldn't fast; it's not good for you. Yet Jesus fasted for forty days and forty nights. And Paul said (1 Corinthians 9:27, in my modern paraphrase), "I keep my body. My body doesn't keep me." I am not advocating abusing your health. We know our bodies are the temples of the Holy Spirit and must be kept accordingly.

So even though the discipline of health is important, it's not the final determining factor. We are so coddled sometimes, over-comfortable, over-concerned with our health. This Western world that is so obsessed with physical appearance needs to look at Jesus and see that he models for us the self-discipline of our bodily appetites. Not only did Jesus have to miss meals on occasions for the sake of his kingdom work, but he was homeless, too. As Matthew 8:20 says, "Foxes have holes, birds of the air have nests, but the Son of Man has no place to lay his head."

Have you ever dealt with homeless people? Have you ever thought about the fact that Jesus was homeless? For thirty years he had a bed of his own and then for three years he didn't. Being without a bed of your own for three years—now *that* would get to you. Sometimes he had somebody else's bed; Martha and Mary gave him one in their home, as well as other hospitable people who welcomed him and believed in his cause. But probably most times he and the disciples were outside under the stars, which sounds glamorous until *you* do it. A friend of mine did it out of necessity once in a desert in Africa, and he was told to get a big stone to put under his head. He said, "You must be kidding." And they answered, "We are not kidding. That's for the ground snakes." So he got a stone and put his head on it! He told me that it is *not* a fun thing to have a stone for a pillow. Jesus knew a lot about that.

> It is not a fun thing to have a stone for a pillow.

"That's not balanced," I hear people say today. And in our eyes it doesn't seem to be. But that was the way Jesus lived.

## A Modern Hero

As I was writing a series of children's books on heroes of the faith, my assignment took me to Holland. The first book was about Corrie ten Boom. Corrie was a brave single lady who, together with her family, hid persecuted Jews from the Nazis who were trying to exterminate them during World War II. Her whole family was betrayed and sent to the death camps.

| Jesus was homeless. |

In Holland we had the privilege of going to her house. What a joy to be there and to stand in the "hiding place," the cupboard in Corrie's room that led to the secret space where Jews were hidden. I took my little black book out and scribbled lots of notes as the guide described the whole operation.

One thing that I didn't know about was the factory Corrie lived in after the war was over. Corrie's sister Betsy had had several dreams in the concentration camp. One: that they would have a home for the mentally retarded, because those were some of the people the Gestapo were torturing and experimenting on. Two: that they would have a place for defectors who were being tarred and feathered after the war. And three: that they would have a place for war victims to recover. They would work to help these people learn to forgive their enemies through discovering the love of Christ.

So when the war ended, all of this came true, and the family home became the place where they took in the collaborators. They filled it with these people who were hated and tried to help them rehabilitate. Corrie fulfilled the visions Betsy had seen. "God will even give us a concentration camp. One of these awful hellholes," Betsy had whispered. And she added, "Corrie, put some flowers in the windows and paint the prison bright." So after the war was over Corrie went to Germany to minister to the very people who had done these dreadful things to them.

At that time the German people were living in broken, bombed-out houses, and Corrie was staying in a little hotel nearby. One day she went back to her hotel after speaking to these hundreds of people who were living in this factory, homeless and hungry—and God said to her, "How can you go and talk to these people and come back to your nice little hotel at night?" So she checked out and moved into the factory and for months lived with the homeless. She was in her sixties, and yet she became like one of them. And during that time a lot of Christians came and tried to dissuade her. They said, "Corrie, this isn't balanced." But God looks at balance very differently than we do.

While Jesus was at home in Nazareth, his family considered him to be balanced, but as soon as he left home and began his sacrificial lifestyle and ministry, his family had lots to say about it. Many other people thought that the way he treated his family was quite wrong, too. In fact, look at Mark 3:31:

> Jesus' family really thought he had lost it!

> Jesus' mother and brothers arrived. Standing outside, they sent someone in to call him. A crowd was sitting around him, and they told him, "Your mother and brothers are outside looking for you." "Who are my mother and my brothers?" he asked. Then he looked at those seated in a circle around him and said, "Here are my mother and my brothers! Whoever does God's will is my brother and sister and mother."

His family really thought he had lost it, because verse 21 says,

When his family heard about this ["this" being that he
didn't have time to eat, wasn't looking after himself proper-
ly], they went to take charge of him.

And the word "charge" means to put him in constraints.
There's only one sort of person you put in constraints and
that's somebody whose mind is unbalanced. So they were
saying in effect, "Poor Jesus. We'd better go and bring him
home." They went to take charge of him by force and to put
him in constraints.

Thus we know from the Scriptures that Jesus himself did
not appear to be very balanced. But of course Jesus—who
always pleased God—was, according to his heavenly Father,
perfectly balanced every day of his life! So what were the
balancing factors for him?

## What to Know, How to Know It

As I thought through the gospel narrative it seemed that three
things were certainly balancing factors for Jesus. They could
be summed up in three phrases that he used concerning his
inner motivation: *I must be about my Father's business; I must do
always those things that please him;* and *I've
finished the work you gave me to do.*

> Ending a
> life at 33
> doesn't
> seem
> balanced.

When my eldest son became thirty-
three, it was a real reminder to me that
that was how old Jesus was when he died.
Thirty-three is so awfully young. Ending a
life at a young age doesn't seem very
balanced, does it? But at the end of Jesus'
life he said, "I've finished the work you gave me to do." Thirty
of those thirty-three years he had in which to accomplish his
"work" he spent in Nazareth.

> *Faith is like a toothbrush. Every person should have one and use it regularly, but he shouldn't try to use someone else's.* —J.G. Stipe

That doesn't seem like an efficient use of his time, does it? But apparently those thirty years in Nazareth were extremely important because God planned that he should spend them there. This was what the King wanted him to put first.

Nazareth living was part of the work the Father had given Jesus to do. After that he spent three years on the road, arriving at Calvary in time to achieve our redemption. Then he went back to heaven and said to his Father, "I've finished the work you gave me to do."

It's a great release to know that the secret to "doing it all" is not necessarily *doing it all*, but rather discovering which part of the "all" he has given us to do and doing all of that. There is something specific set before each one of us, and God will prepare us for that and help us carry it out, even if it means living in "Nazareth" most of our lives!

**Are we finishing the work God gave us to do?**

Remember: there is only so much of the Father's business that he's given *you* to do—and we shouldn't be doing anyone else's part.

So, what is the Father's business for *you*? Over the years I've read a lot of books. I've read books about how to find that priority, and I've read books that say God first, family second, church last. Or again, put church first, family second, and God last! I've written articles myself on the subject. I've taken many positions, all with scriptural foundation!

I've also tried to figure out what various verses in Scripture really mean. For instance, what does it mean when Jesus says, "If anyone comes to me and does not hate his father and mother, his wife and children, his brothers and sisters, yes even his own life, he cannot be my disciple" (Luke 14:26)? Obviously it doesn't mean you really *hate* them; the writer is using comparisons. Compared with the love we have for God, our love for our loved ones should "appear" as if it were hate. But what does that actually mean?

I've come to the conclusion in my old age that it means I put love for God before all my other loves. The priority principle is: first the King and kingdom things. First the King's business. We must "seek first his kingdom and his righteousness" (Matthew 6:33). What that means is whatever the King says is first *today* must be first today. Maybe the things that are first today may not be first tomorrow or the next day, but all I need to worry about is today. His priorities must be our priorities.

> Do whatever the King says is first priority today.

So the King might say, "First for you today is to stay home with your children." Then do it. Have the courage to do it. Or again he might say, "Leave your children in someone else's care today and go and teach a Bible study" or "Go and do this or that." Do it then, if that's what the King says is first today. But don't be surprised if he is telling the person next to you in church to do something else!

How could he possibly tell us all the same thing, anyway? We're all so very different. And we're all in different seasons of life. We all have different responsibilities. So we shouldn't look at someone else and say, "They should be putting 'this' or 'that' first," for we cannot know that. We just need to know it for ourselves.

> *The lordship of Christ, if you take Him seriously,
> will guide you around many of the temptations
> and decisions over which
> most believers agonize.*—Robert A. Cook

## Jesus First—and the Rest Will Come

If you can understand what God wants you to do and when, then everything else will fall into place. A friend of mine loves to say, "If Jesus is first you'll know what's next!" She's right.

You really will. Partners must help each other with this: that's what partners are for—*heirs together* in the King's business so that we can make a dent in enemy territory as a couple. We're supposed to be about the Father's business *together*. And if that is our family focus he will give us a sense of sureness of direction.

> If Jesus is first, you'll know what's next! And you can make a dent in enemy territory.

But along with the fulfillment of such a lifestyle, there's also stress. And most of the stress comes when you get criticized for what you're doing. Looking back over fourteen years of missionary work and twenty-one years as a pastor's wife, I find that the things that knocked me off my feet more than anything else have been (and continue to be) the criticisms of other Christians. Living with disapproval can drain you of all your good resolves to put the King first.

Living with disapproval isn't easy. It could be church disapproval. Or it could be family disapproval. Jesus had to live with both.

I remember when Pete was fourteen, Judy sixteen, and Dave eighteen. Dave was working and Judy was visiting friends for the summer, and Stuart and I were going to South Africa for ministry. We thought it would be great if Pete went home to England during that time. The plan was that I would take him to England and see my mother, and then join my husband in South Africa.

I have always felt pulled in five different directions at once, because of the nature of our ministry. That's been the unusual lifestyle to which God has called Stuart and me. And never more than this particular summer. I remember thinking, *Who am I supposed to be available to this time? My daughter? My eldest son? Stuart? Should I put my children, my husband, or myself first? Do I do what the church wants me to do with my husband in South Africa? And what about my own mother? She's three thousand miles away, not in good health, and who knows what's going to happen to her while I'm so far away?*

And so I tried to figure out what on earth the King was saying should be first. After much prayer we came to the conclusion that I should go with Stuart. So I set off for England, spending some time with Pete and my mother, planning to leave our youngest son there and travel on to join my partner. I had a wonderful two or three days with my mom and Pete and with my sister's three boys who were not then committed believers.

| Living with disapproval isn't easy. | The night before I left England to go to South Africa, Pete came into my room, sat on my bed, and started to cry. He said, "I don't want you to go." |
|---|---|

*Oh no!* I thought. Then I said, "Pete, don't do this to me. I have to go."

Pete had been excited to be home in England, but he was fourteen years old at the time, and it was a difficult time for him. "I don't want you to go," he repeated stubbornly. "I don't want to stay here without you. It's not like I thought it would be. It's strange to me. Please take me with you."

I said, "Pete, I can't take you to South Africa. You don't even have a visa. Even if it were possible to get one I couldn't take you. And I can't stay here. I have to go."

I had been reading in the book of Exodus about the cloud that led the Israelites through the wilderness by day and the pillar of fire that led them by night. I'd been thinking about how the Jewish families must have felt during that experience. I'm sure they got quite fed up with this little cloud because they'd just get the whole family settled into their sleeping bags and get the tent set up when the cloud would take off again. I can hear the dad of the family saying, "Oh no, it's going!" And Mom would be bound to say, "Oh, I can't believe it. I just got the kids to bed." "Get them up, get them dressed," Dad would order. That cloud/pillar certainly was teaching them obedience.

I had made a note in my Bible beside that story, that the blessing of the children lay in the obedience of the parents. I'd just written this down before Peter walked into my room. And so I knew what was supposed to be my first priority: my trip to South Africa. I knew not just through that Scripture but through many other circumstances as well. I knew that I was doing the right thing. But do you know how hard that was for me? All the doubts of what could happen to Pete swam before my mind: Would he get over this? Would he see this as abandonment? Would he resent God for taking us away?

> The blessing of the children lay in the obedience of the parents.

I set off on that five-week tour with a heavy heart, and it was two long weeks before I got a note from Pete. I looked for it every day, but the mail took forever, it seemed, to catch up with me. When the letter finally came, I tore it open. It said something like this:

Thanks to you, and [he had drawn a finger pointing up to heaven] You Know Who, I'm fine. Let me tell you what happened, Mom. Sorry you left me in tears, but they soon dried up and I went to play football with the cousins. Auntie Shirley must have realized I was a little down and she said, "Pete, would you like to go to Capenwray? Wouldn't you like to visit the conference center where you grew up?"

Take note—my sister, up to that point, had hardly heard my husband or me speak. She wasn't sure what we really do. But there she was: offering to take my child to the Christian mission where we had served years ago. And what's more, she had decided her boys would go along. So off they all went to help Pete feel better, and when they got there the leaders greeted them all warmly and invited the boys to stay with them. All three boys came to understand and appreciate the Christian faith. And Pete was there to see it.

Can you imagine getting a letter like that, after it had been so painful to be obedient? I couldn't help coming back to that promise in Scripture, "The blessing of the children lay in the obedience of the parents," and worshipping!

> It takes courage to disappoint people, especially those you love.

Now that does not always mean the mother takes off or the father takes off. The Lord might just as well have said, "You stay put in England." And then I would have had a hard thing to do the other way around. I would have had to cable my husband and tell him to cancel all the meetings that were set up for me. I would have had to tell him, "I really think this is the thing to do. This is what the King is saying is first."

It takes courage to disappoint people, especially those you love. When you don't know what to do, seek God's help. He is intent on letting you know the best way. And when you know what you are supposed to do and follow it, he honors your obedience.

## Shifting Roles

That's the struggle. It would be much easier if you could just buy into a system. We've all done that, haven't we? This book says this and that person says that, or this tape I listened to says something else. We've all bought into behaviors due to our cultural Christian heritage or from whomever or whatever we've learned our behavior patterns. But the harder thing to do is to say, "Lord, you show me what to do today—as a mother, as a wife, as a disciple of yours—in all of these roles that I have."

Let's look again at Peter and his wife. Think about it. This little Galilean homespun girl didn't marry a preacher, did you notice? She married a fisherman, and then he took off and went into the ministry and became the head of the church. Can you imagine what that must have been like for her? (Or maybe you know firsthand!) It must have been a huge shock to her system. Peter and his wife would have been poor. She would never have been to school. She was probably not accustomed to being in the limelight, and here she finds herself thrust into the incredible role of being an apostle's wife!

A young seminary wife confided in me one day:

"I'm frightened."

I responded, "What are you frightened of?"

"I've discovered something about myself that is awful. I'm allergic to people."

I laughed, hard. But she was not laughing. She was feeling quite desperate.

She went on, "I don't like people. How can I be a pastor's wife if I'm allergic to people?"

> "I'm allergic to people."

I said, "You're not allergic to people. You're just more inclined to facts and practical matters."

She's a very gifted woman, a physician's assistant, who has real administrative gifts. In her job she knew she was a people person, but she didn't perceive herself that way in private. "Maybe these are not your main gifts," I continued, "but you'll develop them like everyone else. Don't worry about it. You're not allergic to people."

What she was doing was looking at some primarily people-oriented people around her and saying, "I'm not like them."

And she was right—she wasn't. I told her, "No, you're not like them. You're like you. You're 'different.' Not better—or worse. You're 'different,' and different is beautiful! God will use your difference for him."

Like Peter's wife, this lovely young seminary student hadn't envisioned herself in the position, and she was fearful that her gifts did not fit her role. But as Peter's wife adjusted, so did she. It wasn't so hard. She discovered God had all of this in mind when he "knit her together in her mother's womb."

## Strong Roots

Let's get back to Peter and his wife. How long were they married, do you think? We don't know. Let's guess. Maybe ten years. Living in Galilee; everything was fine. Then what happened? The time came when Jesus walked into her life and walked off with her husband for those three tumultuous years. There were no apologies apparently. Off they went. There were no phones and no possibility of coming home for weekends. And there she was—left with all the home responsibilities. She wasn't a part of the ministry then. Other women—wealthy women—were with Jesus and Peter and the other disciples, supporting

> Jesus walked into her life and walked off with her husband for three years!

them out of their own means (Luke 8), but I don't think Peter's wife was among them.

One of the things I hear constantly from ministry wives is that they have to share their husbands with other people. Often other women spend more time with their husbands in the course of ministry than they do! One pastor's wife told me, "I feel the ministry is like a mistress!" Have you ever felt like that? Sometimes the man needs to be alerted to a hidden danger in this regard, and it's the wife's responsibility to do that. Other times Jesus will speak to our jealous hearts and help us to leave our feelings with him.

So what happened to Peter's wife after those three years of separation? Well, in the Acts of the Apostles we find them together again and, as Paul tells us, Peter and his wife are on the missionary circuit together, going about their Father's business. So this is their pattern: so many years together, so many apart, so many years together again. That's what God had in mind for them. You look at the other apostles and wonder if they had always been together with their wives. Some of them may have had no time apart at all, just a pattern of ministry together.

Then there's the pattern for Jesus: thirty years in Nazareth attending primarily to the needs of his family, and then three years of ministry. The relationships of God's forever family took precedence over Jesus' own family relationships during this period. One of the hardest things for Jesus must have been to let other members of his family care for his mother. And then came the cross, and he had to let someone else look after her again. Can you imagine how that must have felt to Jesus, staying on the cross and letting someone else do the job he had done all those years—and could have done again if he had liberated himself? He must have

> In one sense Jesus had to abandon his earthly family in order to establish a heavenly one.

wanted to come down from the cross for many reasons but especially for that one. In one sense, he had to abandon his earthly family in order to establish a heavenly one. He had to put them through a dreadful ordeal, by choice.

He said to John. "Here is your mother," and to Mary, "There is your son." The relationships of the Father's kingdom took precedence at that point *because the King dictated it*. He stayed on the cross because that's what the King said was first for him. Occasionally that's what will happen in our lives. And we have to learn the art of knowing when it's appropriate and when it's right.

Stuart and I had three years together. Then we had ten years of being separated—sometimes up to ten months out of the year. Since that period in our lives we've had twenty-one years "more or less" together, which to us has been like a honeymoon! But when the world looks at our marriage they think it's very unbalanced. They tell us so. After all, what balanced couple would willingly be separated so much? they ask.

We have often been apart. We have served the Lord together—and apart. But there's one thing to keep in mind: Being physically together doesn't mean you're necessarily together! I know a lot of Christian couples who serve the Lord together, yet they're *apart*. Many times Stuart would call me from the other side of the world to tell me, "I'm with you, Honey." He was in Australia and I was in England, but he *was* with me. We were together in focus, in motivation, in purpose—in obedience.

> If the job is to get done, some families will have to pay the price.

And so there is an overarching necessity for each spouse to have his or her relationship and roots strong in God and to be together on this: What the King is telling us as a couple, as a family, is the first thing we need to do. Quite frankly—and this is not something you hear a lot of talk about—if the job is going to get done, some families will have to pay the price to get their part of it done. And it may have to be your family or my family, at some point in time.

## Support for Those Who Obey

I really don't know any other way. You and I are Christians today because somebody somewhere left his or her family to come and bring the gospel to America. An unknown. A Mr. or Miss Nobody. Maybe he or she never got back to the homeland. Maybe they never saw their families again. But you and I know Christ, and we're going to heaven because somebody left his or her own family to make that possible for our families. There are some people in the Christian body gifted by God to be evangelists, missionaries, and traveling teachers. In our modern context, there are all of the above engaging in all sorts of travel who are called to be away from their homes to do kingdom work in order to finish the Father's business.

> You and I are Christians today because someone left his or her family to bring us the gospel.

Our job is to support those families specifically, to pray for them continually and sympathetically, and to fill up that which is lacking while they are away. Above all, we need to encourage them and not criticize them.

A man came a long distance to see me just after Stuart had left for a three-month trip. He was a godly man; in fact he'd been one of the men who had encouraged us to leave the business world and go into the ministry in the first place. That godly man, who we looked up to, came all that way to tell me,

"Jill, this way of life you and Stuart are leading cannot be right. This is unbalanced."

That did not help me. In fact, it just about finished me off because I was struggling anyway with what I needed to do, what I *knew I had to do.*

That very day a marvelous Canadian missionary happened to be visiting me. She'd come to keep me company, knowing that Stuart had just left. She listened very quietly to what this gentleman was saying to me. When he'd left, she said, "You know, Jill, don't worry about it. I know you're concerned about the children. What are they seeing? They're seeing cost and sacrifice modeled. They're seeing two parents who love each other to death and hate to be apart but do it for one reason: it's the right thing to do for Jesus. And these kids are absorbing all that." I dared to believe she was right. I don't think there's any doubt about one of the reasons all our kids are in ministry today. They all modeled after us.

> Your resource for encouragement, courage, and strength is in the care and provision of God.

Just don't expect the world to stand up and applaud. Remember that people thought Jesus was crazy. Not only did he preach a radical message of forgiven sin and new life, he lived radically, too. He drew criticism by just doing what he was supposed to do. When he stayed home and did the expected, he was fine. But as soon as he started the radical stuff they all said, "He's absolutely out of his mind."

So you're not going to get any help from the world or even from church people sometimes. But remember that your resource for encouragement, courage, and strength is in the care and provision of God.

Heavenly Father,

Thank you for your Word and thank you that it is balanced. Help us not take a verse here and a verse there, but guide us as we look at the whole of Scripture. We thank you that Jesus said many things that could appear contradictory until we stand back and look at them as a whole and realize that overarching all of what he said are principles, balance principles that he wrapped around his life. Help us to get the principles straight, the ones he lived by: "I must be about my Father's business. I must do always those things that please him. I must finish the work he gave me to do." Show us how together, with our partners, we can find out what the King says is first. Help us to know what you say and then have the courage to obey—whatever the criticism or however "unbalanced" somebody tells us we are. And if we find that balance we know, dear Lord, that our ministry will be a privilege, and we won't break and we won't burn out because we're doing the work you've called us to do.

For Christ's sake,

Amen.

# ■ For Further Information . . .

*Pulling Together When You're Pulled Apart* by Stuart and Jill Briscoe. Victor Books, 1991.

# 8

# Living with Criticism

FEAR GOD, AND WHERE YOU GO
MEN WILL THINK THEY WALK IN HALLOWED CATHEDRALS.
—*RALPH WALDO EMERSON*

Shortly after becoming a pastor's wife, I found myself in a church meeting where my husband was the object of criticism. He sat there quietly, offering absolutely no defense. *Why doesn't he say something?* I wondered desperately.

After a few more arrows aimed in his direction, I said to myself, *Well, if he isn't going to defend himself, I guess that is what a good Christian wife is for.*

I rose to my feet, made an impassioned, one-minute speech, burst into tears, and rushed from the auditorium. Since that traumatic event, I have done a little better at handling criticism. (That wouldn't be hard, I can hear you say.)

It's difficult when people criticize you, but it's worse when they go after your husband. Sometimes church members don't want to confront the pastor but feel they can pass on their complaints via the pastor's wife because she isn't so intimidating.

Criticism takes many forms. "He's too deep," says one. "He's too shallow," says the next. "He's too dull. My kids are bored," confides another. Do they expect you to say, "Oh, I agree, Mrs. Smith. He bores me to pieces, too"?

Sometimes when I'm listening to someone criticizing my husband, I think, *Has this person forgotten I'm married to the man? How would she feel if I drew her aside by the coat racks to tell her I felt her husband really should smarten up his appearance?*

> Some people pass on their criticism via the pastor's wife.

How do we handle such encounters? Perhaps we leap to our beloved's defense or cut the person off in mid-complaint. I usually feel quite sick or produce a migraine headache within half an hour of such an episode. After thirty years I still wrestle with the unfairness of it all.

> We need to be teachable, pliable, and change-able.

*They don't know how hard he worked on that sermon,* I say to the Lord. Or, *How unfair of her to compare him to that showey television preacher! We don't compare her husband to Ivan Boesky.*

If we find some truth in the criticism (and there is often some truth), we need to be mature enough to own that part of it and be teachable, pliable, and changeable. But when you're in the middle of it, it's not easy.

## Nine Practical Ways of Dealing with Criticism

Here are some of the ways I have learned to cope with criticism.

1. Hold your breath and count to twenty before saying anything at all.

2. Try to listen long enough to let the complainers know they are being heard, and you have understood the problem.

3. As you listen, ask yourself why this person is so upset. Are they under pressure themselves from other quarters, and did your husband happen along at the wrong moment? (Often this is the case.)

4. Let the first thing you say be a quiet and gentle word. "A soft answer turns away wrath" (Proverbs 15:1, NKJV). "Thank you for being so concerned" is one possibility.

5. Try to be objective and impartial. Pretend your husband belongs to someone else—almost impossible, but try anyway!

6. Don't start to reply with a defensive statement. Find a place to agree without being disloyal. For example, you could say, "I understand your children being bored in church, Mrs. Smith. Most children are at that age."

7. Quietly refute any criticism that is unfair or untrue with such statements as, "I'm not sure you've been given the whole story," or "If you knew all the circumstances, I think you'd judge the matter differently."

8. If you feel the criticism is justified, talk to your husband about it. If not, don't mention it. He has enough on his plate without piling it up with sour grapes.

9. Try to send complainers on their way with no new criticism of the ministry wife (you!).

Paul experienced a lot of criticism in his life and ministry. He was able to say, "It is a very small thing that I am judged of you" (1 Corinthians 4:3, NKJV). I'd like to be able to say that, too, when either of us is criticized. It will only be a small thing to me if I believe, as Paul did, that Jesus is the judge and not this particular church member. Knowing the motives of our hearts, God will evaluate all of our ministry as well as our actions and reactions according to his love, knowledge, and understanding.

> God will evaluate all of our ministry.

All of us benefit by committing it to God and leaving it in his hands.

---

*Living the way we assume other people think we should live can be exhausting.*—Ruth Senter

## The Mouse Trap

People have definite ideas about what the pastor's wife should wear. Have you noticed? While I don't believe I should dress for success, or for the church cats who love to call attention to the church mouse's appearance, I am well aware clothing does make a difference.

Conform, and you could be in trouble. When Stuart and I were in youth work in England, I once made the elementary mistake of thinking, *If I don't dress like the kids we're working with, they won't listen to me. They won't think I'm "with it."*

> People have definite ideas about what a wife in ministry should wear.

My efforts were not appreciated, and the young people lost no time in telling me so. "Be yerself," a punk youngster advised me sagely. "Tight pants don't suit yer."

"True, and thank you for being so honest," I muttered in reply.

I once spoke at a luncheon where a color specialist appeared before me on the program. I tuned in to hear her exhort, "Never do this and that." I, who had done exactly "this and that," looked for somewhere to hide. Even my shoes were wrong.

Appearance, I realize, is important. If the audience can't concentrate because of my distracting attire, all my hours of preparation are for naught. But if I look so "beige" they can't find me against the curtains, that doesn't help either.

Soon after our immigration, a leader's wife gazed at me and sniffed disparagingly, "We'll soon get you out of those old English tweeds and into some nice spring fashions." I felt like a rueful refugee and hung my head. I let her take me over and make me over. A few years later, when polyester sank out of sight and I had gained enough self-confidence, I dug out those lovely wool clothes again.

Sometimes it's the little things, like what you wear and what people think of what you wear, that can be great sources of irritation. You can't be a pastor's wife long before realizing that *nothing* in your life is private anymore. Everything is open to others' judgments and speculation—and criticism.

So you might as well decide that some-one will always disapprove. Decide it, choose to live with that inconvenience, and try to focus your energies on larger issues.

> Try to focus on larger issues.

I will never forget visiting a slum church in Manila where six thousand people lived on a few acres of littered ground, with an open sewer flowing through. Among shacks built of corrugated iron and cardboard boxes, a space had been cleared and cleaned where sixty new believers met to worship.

On the walls made of who knows what hung a broken chalkboard bearing the names of those who attended the service the previous Sunday. With each name was a description of the clothes they had worn to the Lord's house—a clean white shirt, a mended blue skirt, black pants, a large scarf. I was deeply moved.

These new Christians wanted their neighbors to see them go to worship Jesus in their best clothes. Clean, like their new hearts. How they managed it I'll never know, but here's a principle we can apply to our own lives.

If you and I knew that what we wore to church would be written down on a board as we entered, what would the record say? An expensive dress (she paid too much), or a shabby mismatch (no taste at all)? Or would the record say suitable, tasteful, modest, in line with the times, but not so far out she draws attention to herself? After all, our souls are dressed in him and that should be reflected in our whole image.

---

Jesus said, "So do not worry, saying, 'What shall we eat?' or 'What shall we wear?' For the pagans run after all these things, and your heavenly Father knows that you need them. But seek first his kingdom and his righteousness, and all these things will be given to you as well." *Matthew 6:31-33*

---

You see, with clothing there is the larger issue of what clothes reveal about you. If you are too particular about how well your earrings match your sweater, then it's possible that you are "running after" fashion as though there were nothing else in life to be concerned about. If a run in your hose ruins your whole worship experience, there's some work that needs to be done in your attitude. On the other hand, if you wear exactly what you want, when you want to, with no regard for others' feelings, then you are abusing the freedom Christ has given you.

We are called in Christ to be free, but we must never be trapped into using freedom as license.

You may have heard the term: Choose your battles. Although I hate to put church relationships into warfare terminology, this saying is worth remembering for people in the ministry.

People can be very petty. They will try to challenge you on a lot of things, politely or rudely, directly or subtly, and if you aren't careful, your life as a ministry wife will be consumed in small battles over small things. I have already mentioned the issue of how people label you, "This is our pastor's wife," as opposed to using your name. That may be an important issue

> Life is too short for pettiness.

to you, whereas toning down your jewelry for the sake of the more conservative faction in the congregation is no more than a nuisance to you. Very well, then, confront people about what they call you but just change the jewelry and let it go. Life is too short for so much of your energy to be expended over petty items. And you will find that when you refuse to be bothered over petty items, eventually others will lose interest in drawing attention to them. (This won't always be the case, but you can hope!)

As a leader, or as a leader's spouse, it will be up to you most of the time to set the tone of life in your congregation. If people see your vision rising above hairstyles and carpet colors to deal with the bigger issues like evangelism and helping the homeless, then some of those people will catch those higher visions.

Yes, there will be times when you feel like the church mouse in a sanctuary full of cats. That may sound crude, but you know the truth of it. But mice are not stupid; neither are they slow. In fact, they are very resourceful creatures! And some cats are more domesticated than others, but most of them purr when they get the right treatment!

Persevere. Remember that people grow up learning patterns of criticism. They see it modeled for them all their lives. Why is it that some churches have such long, ugly

> **Most cats purr when they get the right treatment.**

histories of repeated splits and heated arguments, and lots of dissension in the congregation? This stuff goes back generations in some cases. The only role models these people had were the argumentative, negative members who were there before them. They need fresh models.

Ask the Lord for a dose of his humility. He took a lot of criticism and harsh treatment that he never deserved, and he knew he didn't deserve it. But he also saw that these were people "harassed and hopeless, like sheep without a shepherd." And he figured that it wasn't such a big price to pay to show them a new way to approach life, even if he got spit on and laughed at in the process. To him, giving them a fresh chance at life was worth the cross.

> Remember that the people who attack you are often reacting out of painful need or their own lack of resources.

You aren't Jesus, but as a disciple you are called to share in his suffering. Some of your criticism will be deserved because you won't always be right. At such times it is even more crucial that you respond with humility and listen to what is being said.

Be prepared for the undeserved criticism. Be prepared to feel like a pounced-on little mouse. And remember that these people you are ministering to so often react out of painful need, out of their own lack of resources. It is your privilege to give them a fresh vision, to show them a better way.

> Get a friend to tell you your faults,
> or better still, welcome an enemy who will watch
> you keenly and sting you savagely.
> What a blessing such an irritating critic will be
> to a wise man. What an intolerable nuisance
> to a fool!—Charles Spurgeon

## When You Feel Inadequate to the Task

Have you ever run into someone in your fellowship who tells you that you are not qualified to help people with deep problems?

"You can't really help her," a young woman told me emphatically one day.

"Why not?" I asked, surprised.

"Because you're not the adult child of an alcoholic, you don't come from a dysfunctional family, and you haven't been sexually abused!" she declared triumphantly.

"Are you saying I can only help people if I've had the same experiences they have?" I inquired.

"Exactly," she replied with great certainty.

The lady talking to me had been a great help to many people with broken backgrounds and certainly would be able to empathize since she had suffered some of the same things in her past.

But I persevered. "Was Jesus the adult child of an alcoholic?" I asked her.

"That's different," she replied. "Jesus could help anyone because he was Jesus."

"O.K.," I countered, "but when you're sick you don't look for a doctor who's had all the diseases in the book, or a dentist who's got false teeth, do you?"

"Of course not," she said defensively.

"The doctor knows his field well enough to diagnose and refer to an expert, or prescribe some medicine himself," I said. "The Christian cannot possibly match all of life's experiences, but we can become skilled in diagnosing and referring and also become spiritually mature enough to have a wise word for the wounded. Above all, we can show others how to have a wise word for the wounded. We can show folks how to have a relationship with Jesus, who can help us all to get a new start or break an old cycle."

I thought about this conversation a great deal. I even caught myself wondering if I would have made a better ministry wife if I had suffered a little bit more (I didn't wonder too long in case the Lord heard my thoughts and took me up on it!).

> God will help you be a positive influence in a negative situation.

The lady had a point. Some problems are so deep and complex that they definitely need a specialist, but all of us can ask the Holy

Spirit's guidance to be an encouragement to the discouraged, a help to the helpless, a positive influence in a negative situation—a friend indeed!

Isaiah 50:4-5 speaks of God's perfect servant. It says that he has the tongue of a teacher—or an "instructed tongue"—and that he might *know how* to give a word to the weary.

This *know how* comes as the Lord sharpens the servant's hearing morning by morning. As I keep faith with God, meeting regularly with him, he will give me words to help a hurting world every day of my life. Our words must come out of our worship.

Didn't Jesus himself say, "I do nothing on my own but speak just what the Father has taught me" (John 8:28)? So God will give to me, a servant of The Servant, the tongue of a disciple and the skill of a counselor, even if I am not trained professionally. I love the King James Version here, which says the servant will "know how to give a word in season to him that is weary." If I will do my part as a disciple, I am promised words for the seasons of life—words for teens who have been reckless in the spring of their days, or other people who are weathering the summer heat of heartbreak, or those enduring the autumn aftermath of tragedy, or cold blast of winter woes. This is what ministry is all about!

> What you have to offer is the life of Jesus, not your own expertise.

This is not to denigrate professional help. Our daughter is a psychologist; we work with a psychological resource center and run many support groups and programs for people with deep needs.

But I've never met a damaged soul yet whom I couldn't leave a little richer, a little lighter, and a little more encouraged because I asked the Lord to use me in his or her life.

Be encouraged—what you have to offer is the life of Jesus, not your own expertise. Encouragement cannot harm people—a loving word from you will always help somehow, if even a little, if only for a moment. As ministry wives, our skills and callings are varied, but we can be unceasing encouragers. We are greatly needed!

Lord, forgive us for our huge ability to see the faults
in others before we see our own.

Our eyes—so full of planks of prejudice prevent us
not from seeing motes
of little account
within our brother's eye.

Guilty as charged, we proudly pronounce
—and they may well be—
But oh, dear Lord, what right do we
small measly mortals
have to judge the motives
of men's hearts?

Teach us that there be but one
great throne of judgment and
that it be most thoroughly
occupied by Thy dear self.

And may we through the knowledge of Thy Son
demolished by our sense of
sinfulness
so know our jungle natures' tendencies
we are forced to cry, "Oh God, be merciful to me,
a sinner!"

And may the tolerance that
mercy births
precipitate a caring of the heart
producing prayers
set free from
judgment chains that change a
world—
our world!
Our troubled, tumbled, truculent, terrible,
tantalizing, touching world!

A world of moms and dads and little ones
fighting for their families—
Oh, may they win!
Hold them together, Lord,
Hold them fast,
prevent them from blowing up their lives
with the devil's dynamite.

Give us grace to tell them—Jesus makes the
difference!

Amen.*

*"Prayer" reprinted from *Heartbeat,* © 1991 by Jill Briscoe (Harold Shaw Publishers).

# ■ For Further Information . . .

*Loving Confrontation: How One Church Discovered the Biblical Principles* by Beverly Caruso. Bethany House Publishers, 1988.
Through the use of anecdotes and twenty-five years of pastoral experience, Bev shares biblical methods of healing relationships within and without the church. A hands-on book to help you discover principles for building strength within your family and church. Packed with practical guidelines for helping the body of Christ to be "fitly joined together" in unity.

# 9

# Renewal on the Run

NO ONE EVER GRADUATES FROM BIBLE STUDY
UNTIL HE MEETS ITS AUTHOR FACE TO FACE.
—*EVERETT HAIRES*

Here's a sobering statistic: according to that survey I mentioned in the beginning of the book, forty percent of ministry wives never have a quiet time. Why? For many reasons. But one of the reasons will be *they never have*. They don't know how. And now that they're ministry wives, who are they going to ask?

The more involved we get in the ministry, the harder it is to ask some elementary questions. "I was raised in a Christian home and they presumed I knew all these things," a girl married to a parachurch worker said to me. "But I don't know how to dig deeper on my own. I don't know how to get a message from the Bible to give to someone else. I don't even know how to put together a little five-minute devotional. Nobody's ever told me that, taught me that. And what's more, I don't know how to get answers from the Bible to my own heart questions."

> People presume we know everything.

This is where humility comes in. That ministry wife had the beautiful quality of humility that enabled her to admit her need. Let's be "small enough to be big enough" to ask for help! A very well-known preacher, when he left seminary, made a list of twenty men he admired. He wrote to them all and said, "I want to learn the secret of your effectiveness. If I get myself to where you are (and they were all over the United States), would you give me one hour of your time?"

That's an example of humility with a purpose. Can you imagine any of those men turning down an offer like that? With that kind of hunger to learn?

So put away the notion that you should have figured out all of this information magically over the years, that it was supposed to float down from heaven and descend upon you when your husband and/or you got ordained or commissioned for special service. It doesn't happen like that. As Jesus said, "Ask and it will be given to you; seek and you will find; knock and the door will be opened to you" (Matthew 7:7).

## Escape from Busyness

We can all relate to the ongoing need for renewal in the midst of our busy day. However, we are often on the run from early morning till late at night and can't seem to find the precious minutes to *be still*. Over and over again ministry wives tell me what an ongoing struggle this is for them. I quite understand; it's an ongoing struggle for me, too!

In Luke 10 we meet Martha, who was seemingly too busy to be blessed. Jesus did not rebuke her busyness but rather her anxiety about it. Jesus wanted to take her worry about her work away from her, relieving her of the stress that is so often the straw that breaks the camel's back. Martha's problem is often ours. We are *distracted by our much serving* and become, as someone has said, *more concerned with the work of the Lord than the Lord of the work!*

> It's easy for us to be like Martha— too busy to be blessed.

It is so easy to do. There was nothing wrong with Martha's

love and devotion for Jesus. But busyness that hustles out to meet the day without meeting Jesus first is busyness that will soon be busy bossing everyone around, getting irritated, becoming self-righteous and downright hostile with everyone in sight. What's more, it is an activity that will end up in an accusing, "Lord, don't you care that my sister has left me to do the work by myself? Tell her to help me!" (Luke 10:40b).

Of course he cares! He would have us join Mary at his feet so he can tell us how much he cares. You might be tempted to think it was easy for Mary. She was obviously of a very different temperament than her sister. But we must be careful; we must not presume we really know what Mary's temperament was like. John Calvin points out that Jesus said she had *chosen* the better part. If this was the case, he suggests, perhaps she was *Martha before she was Mary*. That's a neat thought. Maybe Mary was even more of a Martha than Martha! The point is, whatever our temperament or inclination to worship, we *all* need to make a daily choice to meet him sometime, someplace that fits our particular schedule. If we do, we will go out to serve with his blessing resting on our service, his peace in our hearts, his joy on our lips. If we don't take time to be renewed, we'll end up earning a rebuke at the end of the day.

> Jesus would have us join Mary at his feet.

> We all need to make a daily choice.

So come ye apart and rest awhile—as Jesus invited you. If you don't, you may well find yourself coming apart!

## Practical Ideas for Battling Busyness

May I offer some practical ideas for battling busyness and setting time aside for you and your Lord?

1. Take your calendar off the wall and find the *best* time (it will probably be different each day) to meet with the Lord. Write it on your schedule and then keep your appointment.

2. Start with 15 minutes a day (don't be overly ambitious).

3. Have a plan. Select a short portion of Scripture as something to remember and write it down in a notebook. Record written prayer requests—if you don't know where to start, try the epistles—Philippians maybe.

4. "Be still" and know that he is God—sometime during this exercise.

5. Be faithful—and if you are, you will be blessed. Then it follows that if you are blessed you will be bound to be a blessing!

> Take time
> to be still
> and know
> the Lord.

There are lots of books out, lots of aids for the devotional life—books of prayers, of inspirational thought, of plans to follow for reading through the Bible or going through a certain curriculum of topics. These things can be helpful; use them. But don't lose the real emphasis: time to be still and know the Lord.

## Losing Our Cutting Edge

How easy it is to lose the *cutting edge* of our Christian life—even when we are living in a Christian environment. There was a young man in a school for believers who did just that. The principal of the school was Elijah, and enrollment was so healthy that expansion was planned. All the students set to work to help.

There was one young man who borrowed an axe (a very precious implement in those days) and set about felling trees to clear a plot of ground by a river for the new buildings. He went to his task with great enthusiasm, but suddenly the axe head flew off the handle and fell into the river. He had lost his *cutting edge.*

"Oh Master," he cried to Elijah, "it was borrowed." Elijah took a piece of wood, threw it into the river, and the axe head floated to the top.

At different times in our lives we lose our cutting edge for one reason or another. In my own experience, I have found my life singularly ineffective for many reasons. For instance, it has been easy to rely on Jesus' friends instead of on my friend Jesus. I love to work for the Lord but can become so absorbed that the Lord of my work comes last on my agenda! The quiet time fades into the background. The prayers grow sporadic. Lack of time in God's presence leads to a lack of trust in his promises. Lack of trust soon translates into lack of power; and fear, instead of faith, has left me clutching an "axe handle" with no potential at all.

> It is easier to rely on Jesus' *friends* instead of being friends with Jesus.

I have also discovered that I need to apply a piece of wood shaped like a cross to my helplessness at these times to bring the sharpness back to my Christian life and witness. Christ died to make me fit for heaven but lives to make me fit for earth. As surely as his death brings life to my soul, his life brings a razor-sharp impact to my daily doings. It is up to me, however, to put out my hand and appropriate the cutting edge as he brings it within my reach again.

Whenever you become conscious that you are "blunt," ask yourself, "Where did I lose my edge?" Like the young man in the story, go back to that place and express to your heavenly Elijah (Jesus Christ) your sorrow and repentance for losing such a precious thing. He will make the iron float if you ask him. Ask the Lord to help you do whatever it takes to get that

edge back where it belongs. "Blunt" believers will never accomplish the work the Lord wants done.
They will only succeed in damaging
everyone around them and bringing grief
to the Savior's heart.

> "Blunt" believers will never accomplish the work of the Lord.

That cutting edge is a matter of grace; it
is a gift from God. And we receive gifts
when we are in his presence. The devotional time you spend with the Lord not
only sustains you through the trials and
triumphs of being a ministry wife, but it makes the difference
between your being effective or ineffective.

### Personal retreats

Although it was never an easy thing to do, Jesus had times of
retreat. And if the Son of God needed to retreat sometimes,
how much more do we?

A retreat can simply be a morning at your breakfast table
over the Bible and a pot of tea. Sometimes just a half hour's
peace is all you need.

A retreat is a physical as well as a spiritual exercise. A
doctor told me years ago, "Jill, your heart is bigger than your
body, and you'd better realize that." He was a family friend, a
dear friend. And he was an atheist. But he cared for my health
and kept me going, because my heart *is* far bigger than my
body, and I've had to learn to respect that. So remember that
spiritual renewal involves the body as well. Your body is a
temple of the Holy Spirit. In the chapter "Finding a Balance" I
mentioned that there are times when you have to live in an
unbalanced way, and you do—going short on sleep and nutri-
tion sometimes. But the bigger picture is a person at rest in the
Lord, a person who respects the whole of who she is. And that
whole includes physical, mental, emotional—as well as what
is obviously "spiritual."

So retreat can take on various meanings, and all of them ultimately relate to how your spiritual life is. A walk in the woods, a day to yourself in a motel room or a friend's quiet home, no phones to bother you—be aware and be creative. The Lord can have some real treats up his sleeve if you ask him to give you an idea of how you can retreat to renew!

Today, in America, spiritual retreats are well-known among all types of people, Christian and non-Christian alike. In a way, it is fashionable to be "mystical" or "spiritual." We have to be careful and make certain that our activities are under Christ's leadership. But the good part of all this "spiritual" interest in the general population is that there are more resources out there than ever before. There is relaxing music to listen to, locations specified as retreat areas. Roman Catholics have always seen the need for spiritual reflection; many of their retreat centers as well as Protestant ones are available for individuals or groups needing some quiet space to pray and think about their lives. If you so choose, you can obtain a "spiritual director" for that time. What spiritual directors generally do is provide materials to help you focus on a particular aspect. Maybe they assign a certain passage of Scripture for you to meditate on. These places have lots of materials to help guide prayer time. This type of experience isn't everyone's cup of tea, and all the directors and programs in the world can't substitute for your own listening ear to God's voice. But be aware of the many shapes your devotional life can take, the many ways it can be refreshed.

> Your devotional life can take many shapes.

Sometimes it's a good idea for husband and wife to retreat together, not only to take time to enjoy each other thoroughly on every plane, but to hash through their priorities, the stressing items on their agendas, and take more time to pray than

usual, concentrating on personal, family, and ministry struggles or challenges. For some people, the focus is to regroup
and reorganize; other couples simply need
some peace and quiet in which to be still
before the Lord together and pray long
about what's on their hearts. And you
know how impossible peace and quiet can
be to find in the day-to-day business of
ministry. It is essential that you make the time together for
quietness. As in the example of Jesus' life, sometimes you will
have to settle for minimum rather than maximum time to be
with the Lord. Jesus kept aiming for (and hitting) the goal of
quietness before God and oneness with God's vision. How can
you possibly expect to attain Christlike peace and purpose
without spending time as he did?

> Keep
> aiming for
> the goal.

### Bible study
I'm going to say very little here. Again, there are tons of
materials out there to help you study your Bible. Just don't
let anything get in the way of letting God's Word change
you.

A constant temptation with Bible study (and with prayer) is
to give up when you've tried a system and couldn't get consis-
tent with it. So you reorganize, choose an entirely new system,
buy a new notebook, start at a different passage, and fail again
in a few weeks. Satan loves to see us discouraged. So, start
with fifteen minutes. Read anything in the Word you want.
When you fall, pick yourself up again. Throw away the system if it becomes too burdensome. So what if you're already
behind a month in your "read-the-Bible-in-a-year" program?
Just go back to being there every day, with the Lord, in his
Word, asking the important questions: "What part of this
Scripture is for me? What part of your work is *my* work today?
What sins do I need to confess? What is holding me back?
What principle can help me in this area? What encouraging
truth should I remember?"

> *It is not enough to own a Bible;*
> *we must read it. It is not enough to read it;*
> *we must let it speak to us. It is not enough to let it*
> *speak to us; we must believe it.*
> *It is not enough to believe it;*
> *we must live it.*—William A. Ward

There is a wise saying: God doesn't call us to be successful; he calls us to be faithful. Every time you come back to the Word, every time you attempt again to "be still" and know him, that is counted to you as faithfulness in the Lord's eyes. And he will tell you what you need to know.

### Prayer
Prayer is communication with God.

Sometimes prayer is talking to God, telling him your struggles, your pains, your anxieties—or your joys. God becomes the confidante, the friend who will understand perfectly and love completely.

Sometimes prayer is listening to God. Maybe with the Bible open on your lap. Maybe in the silence of your living room in-between kids and neighbors and housework or while feeding a newborn baby. Most of us are not good listeners; we need more practice at this part of prayer.

And sometimes, prayer is something that cannot be heard or uttered. The Bible says that the Holy Spirit prays for us when we can't pray for ourselves. When all we have inside us is a huge sigh of discouragement, then just be still and sigh! Then think about him praying for

When we pray, God becomes our confidante.

you about it. Sometimes we cannot pray in the forms that have always been expected and acceptable. We can be as honest as we like, transparent before the Lord, and we won't be rejected.

If all we have to offer is a groan or a scream, that is a prayer he'll gladly interpret and answer. When we are in severe emotional pain, it may be virtually impossible for us to have the emotional coherence to pray a "coherent" prayer. We may not have a single "nice" thing to say to God. Maybe all we can say is "Help!" or, "You hurt me!" Maybe all we can utter is the name of Jesus. And that's all right. Utter it!

> *Prayer is the peace of our spirit,*
> *the stillness of our thoughts, the evenness*
> *of our recollection, and the calm*
> *of our tempest.*—Jeremy Taylor

The Holy Spirit has a job to do. He has many functions, actually, and one of them is to translate our prayers to the Father. He takes our groans, our screams, our tears, our muddled phrases, and he transforms them into pure offerings. Prayer opens those lines of heart communication to God Almighty. What a release. Unless we learn to grow in the dimension of our prayer life we will never survive, or revive the ministry.

Pray however you can, whenever you can, wherever you can. Pray in the morning and pray in the evening. Pray through the night. Pray in the kitchen and pray in the car. Pray in the chaos and pray in the order. Pray at the high points and pray at the low points. Pray when you can and pray when you can't. Prayer is your lifeline!

**Prayer is your lifeline.**

A person who relies upon God and listens for his voice is in prayer constantly, her heart open and waiting, her questions, her praises, her problems, all placed before God almost instantaneously, as naturally as breathing.

Don't give up praying. And if you have to start again, give God whatever you've got! It will change your life. It won't only renew your spiritual life; it will bring reality into your ministry.

---

Oh, Word of God,
Pound on my soul,
Drench my life and make me whole.

Accomplish that for which you came,
sprinkle my way
with gentle rain.
And if sometimes the Word seems cold,
help me to read
though it feel old,
for ice and snow can melt
with spring,
and in God's time change everything!

Oh, Word of God
produce in me
a bud—a flower—who knows
a tree.
A gentle shade for
those in need,
A place where hungry ones can feed.

A watered
garden
I would be
Oh, Word of God—
rain Thou on me!*

---

*"Word of God" reprinted from *Heartbeat,* © 1991 by Jill Briscoe (Harold Shaw Publishers).

# ■ For Further Information . . .

*Moments with Majesty* by Jack Hayford. Multnomah Press, 1984.
A devotional gift book exquisitely done with calligraphy and arranged in a sequence spanning the twelve months of the year. Dr. Hayford discusses themes such as expectation, comfort, praise, and growth. This insight gives readers a perspective that teaches, encourages and inspires.

*Discovery* and *Encounter with God* are excellent comprehensive daily Bible reading programs for adults. For more information, contact Scripture Union, 7000 Ludlow Street, Upper Darby, PA 19082.

*Before You Say "Amen"* by Jill Briscoe. Victor Books, 1989.
A practical workbook on prayer.

*Just Between Us*
—a magazine for ministry wives

Edited by Jill Briscoe and a staff of fellow ministry wives, *Just Between Us* features practical articles, helpful ideas and insights, inspiration, and encouragement. The magazine is also sponsor of the annual National Conference for Ministry Wives.

This quarterly publication is just $14.95 per year and is available by writing to:

Just Between Us
1529 Cesery Blvd.
Jacksonville, FL 32211

or by calling (904) 743-5994.